Zoological and Acclimatisation Society of Victoria

Proceedings of the Zoological and Acclimatisation Society of

Victoria

Report of the annual meeting of the Society

Zoological and Acclimatisation Society of Victoria

Proceedings of the Zoological and Acclimatisation Society of Victoria
Report of the annual meeting of the Society

ISBN/EAN: 9783741136320

Manufactured in Europe, USA, Canada, Australia, Japa

Cover: Foto ©Thomas Meinert / pixelio.de

Manufactured and distributed by brebook publishing software
(www.brebook.com)

Zoological and Acclimatisation Society of Victoria

Proceedings of the Zoological and Acclimatisation Society of Victoria

PROCEEDINGS

OF THE

ZOOLOGICAL AND ACCLIMATISATION

SOCIETY OF VICTORIA.

PROCEEDINGS

OF THE

Zoological and Acclimatisation Society

OF VICTORIA,

AND

REPORT OF THE ANNUAL MEETING OF THE SOCIETY,

HELD 25TH FEBRUARY, 1878.

" Omnis feret omnia tellus."

VOLUME V.

MELBOURNE:

SANDS AND McDOUGALL, PRINTERS, COLLINS STREET WEST.

1878.

LIST OF THE OFFICERS

OF THE

Zoological and Acclimatisation Society of Victoria.

———◦◦⊰⊱⊰⊱◦◦———

Patron:

HIS EXCELLENCY SIR G. F. BOWEN, G.C.M.G.

President:

CHARLES RYAN, Esq.

Vice-Presidents:

F. R. KENDALL, Esq. | COLONEL HUTTON.

Hon. Treasurer:

ALBERT PURCHAS, Esq.

Members of the Council:

CURZON ALLPORT, Esq.	C. M. OFFICER, Esq.
DR. THOMAS BLACK.	WM. ROBERTSON, Esq.
THE HON. J. J. CASEY.	PROFESSOR STRONG.
F. R. GODFREY, Esq.	J. C. TYLER, Esq.
F. G. MOULE, Esq.	H. P. VENABLES, Esq., B.A.

THE HON. SIR SAMUEL WILSON.

Hon. Secretary:

ALBERT A. C. Le SOUEF, Esq.

Assistant Secretary:

MR. W. H. D. Le SOUEF.

Collector:

MR. A. O. SEGERBERG.

Hon. Veterinary Surgeon:

MR. GRAHAM MITCHELL.

Bailiff:

FRANCIS MEAKER.

———

OFFICE OF THE SOCIETY—69 TEMPLE COURT.

CONTENTS.

REPORT OF THE COUNCIL.

THE Council of the Zoological and Acclimatisation Society has much pleasure in submitting its Fourteenth Annual Report to the Subscribers.

The Zoological Gardens have, during the past year, proved a great source of attraction, and have been largely visited by the public, the grounds having been considerably improved and beautified. A Fernery and several enclosures for birds have been added, new walks and flower-beds have been laid out, and some of the cages increased in size.

The Chief Secretary was good enough to place the sum of £2,000 on the Estimates for the present year, for the use of the Society, being an increase of £500 on last year's grant, on its being represented to him that the Society found it impossible, with the strictest economy, to maintain the Gardens, and conduct the other operations of the Society, with a less sum.

The Council was, and still is, anxious to make the Society self-supporting, by making a charge at the gates for admission to the Gardens, but the question is at present undetermined. Were anything like an adequate revenue at the disposal of the Society, which in the opinion of the Council might be raised in this way, much more could be done to increase the Zoological collection, and thereby render the Grounds more attractive.

The Council lately heard with deep regret of the death of Mr. Edward Wilson, the Founder and first

President of the Acclimatisation Society. Mr. Wilson always took a deep interest in the progress of the Society, and from time to time, even to the period of his death, assisted its efforts most liberally; his last gift to the Society, which arrived at the same time as the news of his decease, consisting of two Wardian cases of truffle mould, procured in France for experiment in the colony.

The Council is much gratified at having to record a splendid success in the introduction of Californian Salmon (*Salmo Quinnat*), through the instrumentality and liberality of Sir Samuel Wilson. Some months ago, that gentleman obtained a consignment of 50,000 Salmon ova from San Francisco, which, on arrival in New Zealand, were forwarded by Mr. Firth, the President of the Acclimatisation Society at Auckland, who takes a deep interest in the experiment; on reaching Melbourne, in November last, the boxes containing the ova were at once transferred to Ercildoune, and the eggs, with all possible despatch, placed in hatching-boxes, which had been prepared for their reception. The process of hatching very soon commenced, and the final result has been that many thousands of young Salmon have been placed in the best and most suitable streams of Victoria.

The Council is pleased with the success which has attended its efforts to stock the Watts (one of the principal tributaries of the Yarra) with Trout, which was done in the year 1871. A number of fry having been placed in the river at Healesville and Fernshaw, and it is gratifying to know that the fish have succeeded in a satisfactory way. It was mentioned in last year's Report that Trout had been caught in that stream, and during the past year it has come to the knowledge of the Society that a considerable number have been taken.

The Council has, as yet, been unable to procure a supply of the English Brook Trout alluded to in last year's report, but intends to make a further trial, as that fish would prove most valuable for our smaller creeks.

The Society's flock of Angora Goats still continues at Sir Samuel Wilson's Mount Bute Estate, and their numbers are steadily increasing. The surplus bucks have been disposed of during the past year, for the purpose of crossing with the common goat.

The flock of Ostriches, at Messrs. Officer Brothers' station, Murray Downs, has now increased to 19 in number, and a large increase is anticipated during the present season. There have been many difficulties to overcome in their treatment, but now that experience has been gained the experiment bids fair to become, at no distant date, one of considerable national importance.

The Society's game-breeding operations are proceeding satisfactorily. It is intended at once to enclose the Society's Reserve at Gembrook with a high and substantial fence, for the better protection of the game, which is rapidly increasing.

The Council desires to take this opportunity of cordially thanking the retiring President, Professor Strong, for the able manner in which he has performed the duties of the office. And also to record its thanks to Mr. Charles Ryan, the Hon. Treasurer of the Society.

The Balance Sheets, audited by Mr. Rucker and the Hon. Mr. Langton, are laid before the meeting, showing the Expenditure to have been £2,241 3s. 3d., and the Receipts £2,551 12s. 8d. The apparent balance in favour of the Society is caused ;by the Government financial year ending on the 30th June, and that of the Society on the 1st of January in each year.

According to the Rules, Messrs. Kendall, Venables, and Officer retire from the Council, being the three members who have, within the year, attended the fewest number of meetings, but these gentlemen are eligible for re-election.

It now remains for the meeting (see Rule 13) to elect a President, two Vice-Presidents and a Treasurer.

The Council, in conclusion, desires to record its sense of the efficient services of the Honorary Secretary, Mr. A. A. C. Le Souef, to whose exertions the success of the Society is in a great measure due, and of the various employés of the Society. It also desires to express its thanks to Mr. Graham Mitchell, the Honorary Veterinary Surgeon to the Society.

The election of office-bearers for the ensuing year then took place, with the following result:—President, Mr. Charles Ryan; Vice-Presidents, Colonel Hutton and Mr. F. R. Kendall; Treasurer, Mr. Albert Purchas. Mr. C. M. Officer was elected a member of the Council in place of Mr. S. H. Officer, resigned, and Mr. Venables was re-elected on the Council.

ACCOUNT OF MONIES Received and Paid by the ZOOLOGICAL & ACCLIMATISATION SOCIETY OF VICTORIA,

During the period 1st January to 30th June, 1877.

RECEIPTS.

	£	s.	d.
Cash in Hon. Secretary's hands, 1st January	2	16	0
Half rent of Office	11	0	0
Rent of Refreshment Room	11	0	0
Government Grant	1000	0	0
Subscriptions	150	0	0
Sale of Angora Goats	109	5	0
" Guides to Garden	6	0	0
" Angora Goats' Hair	31	13	4
	£1,321	15	1

PAYMENTS.

	£	s.	d.
Premises	199	10	0
Purchase and Transport of Stock	107	16	7
Food and Forage	202	1	7
Farming Implements	10	4	6
Wages	326	13	0
Office Expenses	116	12	9
Incidental Expenses	55	17	0
Fishery Committee	20	0	0
Printing Account	15	7	9
Interest	2	3	10
Cash in Hon. Secretary's hands, 30th June	1	19	4
Balance at Bank of Victoria, 30th June	84	8	5
Overdraft at Bank of Victoria, 1st January, 1877	178	11	1
	£1,321	15	1

CHARLES RYAN, *Hon. Treasurer.*

ALBERT A. C. LE SOUEF, *Hon Secretary.*

Audited and found correct,

W. F. A. RUCKER, *Auditor.*

MELBOURNE, 13th *July*, 1877.

BALANCE SHEET.

ACCOUNT OF MONIES Paid and Received by the ZOOLOGICAL & ACCLIMATISATION SOCIETY OF VICTORIA,

During the period 1st July to 31st December, 1877.

RECEIPTS.

	£	s.	d.
Cash in Hon. Secretary's hands, July 1st..	1	19	4
Balance at Bank of Victoria, July 1st	84	8	5
Sale of Angora Goats	36	0	0
Rent of Refreshment Room ..	33	0	0
Subscriptions ..	149	19	0
Government Grant ..	1000	0	0
Sale of Mohair ..	11	18	7
	£1,316	5	4

PAYMENTS.

	£	s.	d.
Premises	202	1	2
Purchase and Transport of Stock	92	7	6
Food and Forage	151	6	3
Farming Implements	4	11	0
Wages	314	12	0
Office Expenses	125	19	11
Incidental Expenses	92	9	5
Gembrook Account (Reserve)	22	5	0
Interest	0	3	8
Cash in Hon. Secretary's hands, December 31st	4	5	1
Balance at Bank of Victoria, December 31st	306	4	4
	£1,316	5	4

CHARLES RYAN, *Hon. Treasurer.*

ALBERT A. C. LE SOUEF, *Hon Secretary.*

Audited and found correct,

EDWARD LANGTON, *Auditor.*

MELBOURNE, 21st January, 1878.

LIFE MEMBERS.

—+8◇◇8+—

Aldworth & Co., Sandhurst £10 10 0
Armitage, George, Ballarat .. 10 10 0
Armstrong, W., Hexham .. 10 10 0
Armitage, F. W., Duck Ponds.. 10 10 0
Adams, J. W., St. Enoch ...10 10 0
Alfrey, Ernest, Fernihurst .. 10 10 0
Ayrey, Charles, Warranuke .. 10 10 0
Amess, Samuel, William-street 10 10 0
Armstrong, R. G., Salt Creek .. 10 10 0
Barkly, His Excellency Sir Henry 42 0 0
Bear, Hon. J. P., M.L.C. .. 21 0 0
Bear, Thomas H., Heidelberg .. 10 10 0
Buchanan, A., Lismore 10 10 0
Black, Dr. Thomas, Melbourne
Club 10 10 0
Black, W., Belfast 10 10 0
Borough Council, Sandhurst .. 10 10 0
Box, Henry, Little Collins-street
West 10 10 0
Beaney, Dr. J. G., Collins-street
Boyd and Currie, Collins-street
West 10 10 0
Bright Bros. & Co., Flinders-lane 10 10 0
Brown, Lindsay, Garramadda,
Wahgunyah 10 10 0
Bushell, C., Chiltern 10 10 0
Bowen, His Excellency Sir George 10 10 0
Black, Hon. Neil, M.L.C., Mount
Noorat 10 10 0
Campbell, Finlay, Raywood .. 10 10 0
Chambers, H. J., St. Kilda .. Services
Cooper, Sir Daniel, London .. 37 2 0
Coppin, G. S., Richmond .. 10 10 0
Creswick Borough Council of .. 10 10 0
Colbert, Edmond, Rowena-
parade, Richmond .. .. Services
Cumming, G., Mount Fyan .. 10 10 0
Cumming, W., Toorak 10 10 0
Curr, E. M., Queen-street .. 10 10 0
Calvert, John, Colac 10 10 0
Currie, J. L., Lara 10 10 0
Chirnside, A., Werribee Park .. 10 10 0
Clarke, W. J., Sunbury 10 10 0
Clarke, Joseph, St. Kilda-road.. 10 10 0
Chrichton, A., Berwick 10 10 0

Docker, F. G., Wangaratta £10 10 0
Dalgety and Co., Little Collins-
street 10 10 0
Edols, John, Ingleston 10 10 0
Falconer, J. J., Bank of Austral-
asia 20 0 0
Fellows, The Hon. T. H. .. 10 10 0
Firebrace, R. T. 10 10 0
Fraser, Simon, M.L.A. 10 10 0
Fussell, R. S. R., Fou Chou
(dols. 50).. .. .. .. 11 0 10
Fleming, J. W., Brunswick .. 10 10 0
Fisher, C. B., St. Kilda 10 10 0
Glass, R. J., Waiparella.. .. 10 10 0
Hoddle, R., Bourke street .. 10 10 0
Hoffmann, W., Bush Back,
Essendon 25 0 0
Highett, Miss 10 10 0
Henty, Edward, St. Kilda-road 10 10 0
Hay, W., Boomanoomana,
N.S.W. 10 10 0
Hepburne, B., Ballarat 10 10 0
Jamieson, Hugh 10 10 0
Jenner, Hon. C. J., M.L.C. .. 10 10 0
Jones, Lloyd, Avenel 10 10 0
Joshua Bros., William-street .. 10 10 0
Ibbotson, Charles, Geelong .. 10 10 0
Lyster, W. S., Melbourne .. 10 10 0
Landells, G. J., Lahore, India .. Services
Layard, C. P., Colombo .. .. Services
Layard, E. L., Cape Town .. Services
Lansell, G., Sandhurst 10 10 0
Learmonth, Thomas, Ercildan-
riley, Portland 10 10 0
Londesborough, The Right Hon-
orable Lord, Carlton Gar-
dens, London 37 10 0
Lyall, W. 10 10 0
Latham, E., Carlton Brewery .. 10 10 0
M'Eachern, D., Kangaroo .. 10 10 0
Mein, G. A., Moolpa, N.S.W. .. 10 10 0
Mackinnon, L., Argus Office .. Services
Mackenzie, John, Collins-street 10 10 0
Mackintosh, Alexander 10 10 0
Marshall, Capt. D. S. .. .. Services

Martin, Dr., Heidelberg..	£10	10	0
Matheson, J., Bank of Victoria	21	0	0
McGill, A.	10	10	0
McGregor, Samuel, Belfast ..	10	10	0
McHaffie, John, Phillip Island..	10	10	0
McPherson, Hon. J. A., M.L.A.	10	10	0
McMullen, J., Union Bank ..	21	0	0
McKellar, Hon. T., M.L.C. ..	10	10	0
Molloy, W. T., Hawthorn ..	10	10	0
Mueller, Baron Von, Botanic			
Gardens	10	10	0
Municipal Council of Ballarat W.	20	0	0
Murray, S., Dunrobin	10	10	0
Murphy, J. R., St. Kilda-road ..	10	10	0
Nicholson, Germain, Collins-st.	10	10	0
North Eastern Agricultural and			
Horticultural Society ..	10	10	0
Officer, C. M., Brighton ..	10	10	0
Officer, S. H., Murray Downs,			
N.S.W.	10	10	0
Officer, W., Zara, N.S.W. ..	Services		
Ormond, F., Toorak	10	10	0
Purchas, Albert, Kew ..	105	0	0
Russell, Hon. P., M.L.C.,			
Brighton Road	10	10	0
Ritchie, J., Streatham	10	10	0
Rostron, John R., Navarre ..	10	10	0
Russell, A., Matuwalloch ..	10	10	0
Rutledge, William, Belfast ..	10	10	0
Salmon, J., E. S. & A. C. Bank	21	0	0
Sargood, King, and Sargood,			
Flinders-street	10	10	0
Shoobridge, E., Valleyfield, Tas-			
mania	10	10	0

Staughton, H., Melton ..	£10	10	0
Simson, J., Waverley	10	10	0
Simson, Hon. R., M.L.C., Toorak	10	10	0
Sloan, W. S., Fou Chou (dols. 50)	11	0	10
Spowers, Allan, *Argus* Office ..	10	10	0
Stanbridge, W. E., Daylesford..	10	10	0
Staughton, S. T., Little Collins			
street West	10	10	0
Strachan, J., London Chartered			
Bank	21	0	0
Stewart, J., Emerdale, Streatham	21	0	0
Sladen, Hon. C., Birregurra ..			
Sumner, Hon. T. J., M.L.C.,			
Flinders-lane West	10	10	0
Shaw, Thomas, Jun., Camper-			
down	10	10	0
Taylor, W., Overnewton, Keilor	10	10	0
Templeton, Hugh, Fitzroy ..	Services		
Ware, Joseph, Caramut.. ..	10	10	0
Wilson and Mackinnon, Collins-			
street East	42	0	0
Wilson, Edward, *Argus* Office..	21	0	0
Wilson, Samuel, Ercildoune ..	10	10	0
Winter, James, Toolamba, Mur-			
chison	10	10	0
Winter, Thomas, Winchelsea ..	10	10	0
Winter, S. P.	10	10	0
Ware, J., Yalla-y-Poora.. ..	10	10	0
Winter, W., Stanhope	10	10	0
Wilson, John, Woodlands ..	10	10	0
Wilson, John, Gala, Lismore ..	10	10	0
Watson, J. B., Sandhurst ..	10	10	0
Youl, James A., Clapham Park,			
London	Services		

ANNUAL MEMBERS.

—⟶⟵—

Allport, C., Chancery-lane	..	£1	1	0	Buncle, J., Hotham	..	£1	1	0

Allport, C., Chancery-lane .. £1 1 0
Amess, S., William-street .. 1 1 0
Anderson, A., Tottington .. 1 1 0
Atkin, C. A., Hotham 1 1 0
Ayrey, C., Waranook 10 10 0
Australian Mortgage, Land and
    Finance Company 2 2 0
Adams, J. (of Lawrence and
    Adams), William-street .. 1 1 0
Adams, J. and W., St. Enoch .. 2 2 0
Alcock, H. U., Russell-street .. 1 1 0
Armstrong, Thos., Toorak .. 1 1 0
Anketell, T., Landsborough .. 1 1 0
Buckley and Nunn, Bourke-
    street 2 2 0
Buckley, J., Sandhurst 1 1 0
Bell, Joseph, Garden Gully .. 1 1 0
Buscombe, J. H. K., Kyneton .. 1 1 0
Bowyer, E., Cheavely .. ..· 1 1 0
Banks Bros., Bell and Co.,
    Flinders-lane 2 2 0
Borough Council, Malmsbury .. 10 0 0
Briscoe and Co., Collins-street .. 2 2 0
Black, Hon. Neil, M.L.C., Kew 2 2 0
Baines, E., Little Collins-street 2 2 0
Braithwaite, W., Kyneton .. 1 1 0
Broadribb, K. E., St. Kilda .. 2 2 0
Buckland, C. W., Maldon .. 3 3 0
Barnes, W., Brunswick 1 1 0
Black, Dr. J., Carlton 2 2 0
Blair, James, Toorak 1 1 0
Bright Bros., Flinders-lane .. 1 1 0
Blair, Dr., Collins-street.. .. 1 1 0
Bromby, Rev. Dr., Toorak .. 1 1 0
Bligh and Harbottle, Flinders-
    lane 2 2 0
Buchanan, A., Lesmore 5 5 0
Balfour, Hon. J., M.L.C., Little
    Collins-street 1 1 0
Buckley, E., Newbridge 1 1 0
Bindon, Judge, St. Kilda ..· 1 1 0
Balmer, G., Ballarat 1 1 0
Box, J. B., Temple Court .. 1 1 0
Benn, J., Flinders-lane 2 2 0
Barry, D. M., Brunswick .. 1 1 0

Buncle, J., Hotham £1 1 0
Brown, M. J., Green Hills .. 1 1 0
Blair, W. G., Kyneton 1 1 0
Booth, S., Kyneton 1 1 0
Carr, R., Sandhurst 1 1 0
Crooke, Dr., Gertrude-street .. 1 1 0
Catto, J., East Melbourne .. 1 1 0
Cleeland, J., Bourke-street .. 1 1 0
Clarke, Joseph, St. Kilda-road.. 10 10 0
Clothier, S., Eaglehawk 1 1 0
Crosby, W., and Co., Queen-
    street 1 1 0
Curcier and Adet, Queen-street 1 1 0
Curtain, J., Carlton 2 2 0
Collected by C. W. Buckland,
    Maldon.. .. .. .. 18 10 6
Crair, Thomas, Yarra Bank .. 1 1 0
Cornwell, A., Brunswick .. 1 1 0
Cumming, Hon. J., M.L.C.,
    Toorak 2 2 0
Caldwell, J. F., Eaglehawk .. 1 1 0
Cook, C. P., Lake Condah .. 1 1 0
Carson, J., Collins-street .. 1 1 0
Clarke, J. W., Sunbury 10 10 0
Campbell, J., Ballarat 1 1 0
Cuthbert, Hon. H., M.L.C., Bal-
    larat 1 1 0
Currie, G., Kaarimba 1 1 0
Cumming, W., Toorak 1 1 0
Currie, J. L., St. Kilda.. .. 10 0 0
Chomley, A. W., Temple-court 1 1 0
Chennerry, A., Delatite .. 2 0 0
Chennerry, Mrs., Delatite .. 2 0 0
Cock, R., Kyneton 1 1 0
Carter, W., Kyneton 1 1 0
Christie, L. S., Ballarat .. 1 1 0
Duncan, A., Kyneton 1 1 0
Dempster, A., Royal Park .. 1 1 0
Danks, J., Bourke-street .. 1 1 0
Daley, J., Spring-street 1 1 0
Daws, G. R., Kingstern, Creswick 1 1 0
De Pass Bros., Collins-street .. 1 1 0
Dutton, G., Kyneton 1 1 0
Dixson, R., and Co., William-
    street 1 1 0

B

Dight, W. S., Albury	£1	1	0
Dudgeon and Arnell, Lonsdale-			
street	1	1	0
Easton, A. W., Launacooric ..	1	1	0
Evans, G., *Argus* Office ..	2	2	0
Ellis, J., Royal Park	1	1	0
Fanning, Nankivell, and Co.,			
Flinders-street	2	2	0
Faulkner, Dr., Kyneton.. ..	1	1	0
Frew, G., Royal Park ..	1	1	0
Foy, Mark, Smith-street ..	1	1	0
Finlay, J., St. Kilda	1	1	0
Fraser, Alex., Maldon	1	1	0
Findlay, I., Towong	2	2	0
Fitzgerald, N., M.L.C.	2	2	0
Ferguson, D., Flowerdale ..	1	1	0
Fiskeu, A., Queen-street ..	1	1	0
Felton, A., Flinders-lane ..	1	1	0
Fairchild, J. R., Church-street	1	1	0
Fitzgibbon, E. G., Town Hall ..	1	1	0
Goldsbrough, R., and Co.,			
Bourke-street	2	2	0
Grice, R., Flinders-lane ..	1	1	0
Greenwood and Inman, Eliza-			
beth-street	2	2	0
Giles, A. I., Kyneton	1	1	0
Gibson, R., Royal Park ..	2	2	0
Glew, J., Brunswick	1	1	0
Gunst, Dr., Collins-street ..	1	1	0
Gurner, H. F., Crown Law Office	1	1	0
Graham, Hon. J., M.L.C., Little			
Collins-street	1	1	0
Grant, J., Collins-street.. ..	1	1	0
Godfrey, W., Collins-street ..	1	1	0
Gordon & Gotch, Collins-street	1	1	0
Gray, C., Narebb Narebb ..	5	5	0
Green, J. R., & Co., Gertrude-			
street	1	1	0
Gorden, G. — C.E., Mining De-			
partment	1	1	0
Godfrey, F. R., St. Kilda ..	2	2	0
Greville, C., Custom House ..	1	1	0
Hunt, Thos., M.L.A., Kilmore..	1	1	0
Hart, H. J., Queen-street ..	1	1	0
Hoddle, R., Bourke-street ..	2	2	0
Halstead and Kerr, Elizabeth-			
street	1	1	0
Highett, Hon. W., M.L.C.,;Rich-			
mond	2	2	0
Harper, R., and Co., Flinders-			
street	1	1	0
Henderson, T., Royal Park ..	1	1	0
Haige, H., and Co., Elizabeth-			
street	1	1	0
Howitt, E., South Yarra ..	1	1	0
Hickling, F. J., Warrnambool ..	1	1	0
Henty, E., St. Kilda-road ..	2	2	0

Hepburne, W., Ballarat ..	£1	1	0
Ham, J. T., and Co., Swanston-			
street	1	1	0
Heath, R. M., Kilmore	1	1	0
Hutcheson, Jas., Kyneton ..	1	1	0
Hinsby, F. G., Kyneton.. ..	1	1	0
Hurry, H., Kyneton	1	1	0
Hardie, A., Kyneton	1	1	0
Holdsworth, J., Sandhurst ..	1	1	0
Hadden, F. W., *Argus* Office ..	2	2	0
Horewood, Joel, Sandhurst ..	1	1	0
Hutten, Col., Kew	1	1	0
Ingles, D., Flinders-street ..	1	1	0
Ibbotson, Charles, Geelong ..	2	2	0
Ingamelles, J., Royal Park ..	1	1	0
Irving, J. L., Royal Park ..	1	1	0
Jarrett, H., Kynetou	1	1	0
Johnson, W. X., Kyneton ..	1	1	0
James, J. R., Royal Park ..	1	1	0
Jacobs, F., and Co., Queen-			
street	1	1	0
Johnston, E., Elizabeth-street ..	1	1	0
Jones, H., Gold-broker, Sand-			
hurst	1	1	0
Johnson, G. W., Kyneton ..	1	1	0
Jackson, H., Sandhurst ..	1	1	0
Jackson, G. E., Sandhurst ..	1	1	0
Jones, J. Nelson, Sandhurst ..	1	1	0
James, Dr., Collins-street. ..	1	1	0
Keep, E., and Co., Elizabeth-			
street	1	1	0
King, S. G., Hotham	2	2	0
Kendall, F. R., Little Collins-			
street	1	1	0
Kronheimer, J., and Co., Queen-			
street	1	1	0
Kininmouth, J., Baruna Plains	1	1	0
Knochenhauer, C. E., Swanston-			
street	1	1	0
Kinnear, R. H., Lower Moira ..	1	1	0
Kirkwood, H., Eaglehawk ..	1	1	0
Long, D. R., Bourke-street ..	1	1	0
Lee, B., Bourke-street	2	2	0
Lindley, A. B., Royal Park ..	1	1	0
Larnach, J., M.D., Kilmore ..	1	1	0
Le Souef, A. A. C.	2	2	0
Lewis, W., Beaufort	1	1	0
Lobb, W. J., Brunswick.. ..	1	1	0
Lister, C., Bourke-street ..	1	1	0
Lyell & Gowan, Elizabeth-street	2	2	0
Longford, Dr., Kyneton.. ..	1	1	0
Learmonth, W., Ettrick.. ..	1	1	0
Latham, E., Carlton	1	1	0
Law, Somner, and Co., Swan-			
ston-street	1	1	0
McFarland, R., Bourke-street ..	1	1	0
Mathieson, J., Eaglehawk ..	1	1	0

MacGillivray, Dr., Sandhurst	£1	1	0
Moodie, W., Kilmore	1	1	0
McDougall, J., Carlton	1	1	0
McVean, J., Toorak	1	1	0
McNaughton, Love, aud Co., Flinders-lane	1	1	0
Martin, T., Brunswick	1	1	0
McDougall, C., Brunswick	1	1	0
Martin, G. and Co., Market-street	2	2	0
Matheson, J., Collins-street	1	1	0
Malleson, England, and Stewart, Queen-street	1	1	0
McIlwraith, J., Little Collins-street	1	1	0
McKellar, Thos., Hamilton	5	5	0
Moule, F. G., Market-street	1	1	0
McCoy, Professor, University	1	1	0
Manallack, Thos., Brunswick	1	1	0
McLean, N., and Son, Swanston-street	1	1	0
Maplestone, H., Royal Park	2	2	0
McEwan, Jas., and Co., Elizabeth-street	2	2	0
Munroe, Hon. J., M.L.A., Collins-street	2	2	0
Martin, P. J., Flinders-lane	1	1	0
Michaelis, M., Lonsdale-street	1	1	0
Mitchell, Hon. W. H. F., M.L.C., Parliament House	1	1	0
Miller, E., Market Buildings	1	1	0
Maquirie and Cohen, Conally, N.S.W.	2	2	0
Mackay, J., Kyneton	1	1	0
Murray, W., Kyneton	1	1	0
Moorhead, Captain, Sandhurst	1	1	0
Moore Bros., Sandhurst	1	1	0
Mackay and Co., Sandhurst	1	1	0
Macpherson, L., and Co., Sandhurst	1	0	0
Melbourne 'Bus Company	3	3	0
Madden, J., Chancery-lane	1	1	0
Mack, I., Berry Bank, Cressy	1	1	0
Mousse, Dr.	1	1	0
Menzies, Thos., Kyneton	1	1	0
Nolan, L., Brunswick	1	1	0
Nicholson, Germain, Collins-st.	1	1	0
Overend, B., Brunswick	2	2	0
Officer, C. M., Toorak	2	2	0
Oswald, R., Maldon	1	1	0
O'Connor, T. D., Kilmore	1	1	0
Oldfield, L., Royal Park	1	1	0
Oddie, Jas., Ballarat	1	1	0
Oliver R., Coliban Park	1	1	0
Oliver, G., New Zealand	2	0	0
Osborne, James, Merton Lodge, Elsternwick	1	1	0
Plummer, Dr., Sandridge	£1	1	0
Perry, J., Russell-street	1	1	0
Paterson, Laing and Co., Flinders-lane	2	2	0
Paterson, J., Flinders-street	1	1	0
Peterson, W., and Co., Queen-st.	1	1	0
Ploos Van Amstel, J. W., Collins-street	1	1	0
Pitt, W., Bourke-street	1	1	0
Pearson, J. P., Kyneton	1	1	0
Ryan & Hammond, Bourke-st.	2	2	0
Rosier, J. W., Elizabeth-street	1	1	0
Russell, Hon. P., Melbourne Club	10	0	0
Rogers, J., Kyneton	1	1	0
Rocke, W. H., Collins-street	1	1	0
Rosser, Mrs. C., Brunswick	1	1	0
Robertson, G., Little Collins-st.	1	1	0
Russell, Thos., Baruna Plains	1	1	0
Rowe & Stoddart, Miller's Ponds	2	2	0
Rucker, W. F. A., Queen-street	1	1	0
Robertson, W., Colac	2	2	0
Rudall, I. T., F.R.C.S., Collins-st.	1	1	0
Robertson, Wagner, and Co., Bourke-street	2	2	0
Rodgers, J., Kyneton	1	1	0
Ross, C., Sandhurst	1	1	0
Reade, G., Eaglehawk	1	1	0
Ryley, F., Wangaratta	1	13	0
Stevenson and Elliot, King-st.	1	1	0
Symington, J., Kyneton	1	1	0
Sprigg, W. G., Market-street	1	1	0
Smith, C. and J., Albert-street	1	1	0
Scott, Andrew, Jolimont	2	0	0
Simson, J., Waverley	1	1	0
Sloane, W. and Co., Collins-st.	1	1	0
Swallow and Ariel, Sandridge	1	1	0
Sprigg, G., St. Kilda	1	1	0
Skinner, Judge	1	1	0
Shire Council, Kyneton	10	0	0
Stanford and Co., Bourke-street	1	1	0
Stevens, Thos., Maldon	1	1	0
Sands and McDougall, Collins-st.	2	2	0
Shire Council, Colac	5	0	0
Sargood and Son, Flinders-street	2	2	0
Sanderson, J. & Co., William-st.	1	1	0
Shaw, Thos. Jun., Camperdown	10	0	0
Simson, C. W., Toorak	1	1	0
Skene, Hon. W., Hamilton	2	2	0
Simson, Hon. R., M.L.C., Toorak	2	2	0
Strong, Professor, University	1	1	0
Sharp, J., Collins-street	1	1	0
Smale, A. W., Queen-street	1	1	0
Smith, G., Ballarat	1	1	0
Stillwell and Knight, Collins-st.	1	1	0
Straw, T., Brunswick	1	1	0
Steward, J., Eaglehawk	1	1	0

	£	s	d
Sandhurst City Council	£5	0	0
Sellar, R., Queen-street	1	1	0
Staughton, H., Melton	1	1	0
Sachs, J. G., Elizabeth-street ..	1	1	0
Tinning, J., Brunswick	1	1	0
Terry, A., Royal Park	1	1	0
Taylor, W., Keilor ..	2	2	0
Twentyman, R., Flinders-street	1	1	0
Taylor, T. H., William-street ..	1	1	0
Twentyman, T., Dorcas-street ..	1	1	0
Taylor, J., Kilmore ..	1	1	0
Tyler, J. C., Custom House ..	1	1	0
Thomas, Jas., Kilmore	1	1	0
Thomson, J. C., Kyneton ..	1	1	0
Thunder, A., Sandhurst	1	1	0
Trumble, H., Eaglehawk ..	1	1	0
Taylor, Jas., Californian Gully..	1	1	0
Velter, J., Echuca	1	1	0
Venables, H. P., Education Office	2	2	0
Vahland, W. C., Sandhurst ..	1	1	0
Williamson, Dr., Swan Hill ..	2	2	0
Watson, J. B., Sandhurst ..	5	5	0
Watson, G., Burnet-st., St. Kilda	1	1	0
Wilson, Dr., J.P., Craigieburn..	£1	1	0
Wright, J. and Co., Flinders-lane	1	1	0
Wallace, Hon. J. A., M.L.C., Bourke-street	1	1	0
Warnock Bros., Maldon	1	1	0
Wilson, Edward, *Argus* Office ..	2	2	0
Wilshin and Hurley, Collins-st.	1	1	0
Wood, J., and Son, Collingwood	1	1	0
Welch, H. P., Queen-street ..	1	1	0
Wilson, H., Kilmore	1	1	0
Whitney, Chambers, and Co., Swanston-street	2	2	0
White, J. H., William-street ..	1	1	0
Ware, J., Yalla-y-Poora	10	0	0
Watson, G., Garden Gully ..	1	1	0
Watson, J., Garden Gully ..	1	1	0
Wells, G. E., Garden Gully ..	1	1	0
Weddel, J. G., Sandhurst ..	1	1	0
Wilkins, A., Market-street ..	2	2	0
Webster, G., and Co., Flinders-lane	1	1	0
Wilson, J., Gala	10	10	0

HONORARY MEMBERS.

—►8◇◇8◄—

Allport, Morton, Hobart Town
Blanchard, W., Collins Street West
Bouton, A., Yahoue, New Caledonia
Buckland, Dr. F., London
Chalmers, Dr., New Zealand
Cleeland, J., Albion Hotel, Bourke Street
Coste, Professor, Huningue
Drouyn, de Lhuys, Paris
Francis, Francis, London
Gillanders and Arbuthnot, Calcutta
Godfrey, Captain J. B.
Grote, Arthur, Calcutta
Howitt, Ed.
Johnston, Clement, Crown Lands Office
Jones, Captain, "Superb"
Madden, Walter, Office of Mines
Mathieu, A., Yahoue, New Caledonia
Merryman, Captain, "Essex"
Michaelis, Mouritz, Elizabeth Street
Michael, Major, Madras
McQueen, Captain, "Martha Birnie"
Mullick, Rajendro, Calcutta
Officer, Sir Robert, Hobart Town
Ramel, Monsieur, Paris
Ridgers, Captain, "Sussex"
Robinson, J., Calcutta
Salt, Sir Titus, Saltaire, England

Scholstein, Adolp., Flinders Lane West
Sclater, Dr. P. L., London
Shinner, Captain, "Northumberland"
Smith, Captain, "Dover Castle"
Squire, Surgeon John, Dinapore
St. Hilaire, G., Bois de Bologne, Paris
White, J. H., Collins Street West
Conrad, Captain, "Herzog Ernst"
Grant, Charles Lyall, Shanghai
Stacpool, Captain, "Shannon"
Cooper, Captain, "Carlisle Castle"
Consul for Austria
    ,,   Belgium
    ,,   Brazil
    ,,   Chili
    ,,   Denmark
    ,,   France
    ,,   German Empire
    ,,   Hawaii
    ,,   Italy
    ,,   Netherlands
    ,,   Peru
    ,,   Portugal
    ,,   Russia
    ,,   Spain
    ,,   Sweeden and Norway
    ,,   United States

THE RULES AND OBJECTS

OF THE

Zoological & Acclimatisation Society

OF VICTORIA.

1. The objects of the Society shall be the introduction, acclimatisation, liberation, and domestication of innoxious animals and vegetables, whether useful or ornamental;— the perfection, propagation, and hybridisation of races newly introduced, or already domesticated;—the spread of indigenous animals, &c., from parts of the colonies where they are already known, to other localities where they are not known;—the procuring, whether by purchase, gift, or exchange, of animals, &c.;—the transmission of animals, &c., from the colony to England and foreign parts, in exchange for others sent thence to the Society;—the collection and maintenance of zoological specimens, for exhibition or otherwise;—the holding of periodical meetings, and the publication of reports and transactions, for the purpose of spreading knowledge of acclimatisation, and inquiry into the causes of success or failure;—the interchange of reports, &c., with kindred associations in other parts of the world, with the view, by correspondence and mutual good offices, of giving the widest possible scope to the project of acclimatisation;—the conferring rewards, honorary or intrinsically valuable, upon persons who may render valuable services to the cause of acclimatisation.

Membership. 2. A Subscriber of one guinea or upwards annually, which shall be payable in the month of January, shall be a Member of the Society; and contributors, within one year, of ten guineas or upwards shall be Life Members of the Society; and any person who may render special services to the Society, by contribution of stock or otherwise, shall be eligible for life membership, and may be elected as such by the Council, or by any annual general meeting.

Property vest in the Council. 3. All the property of the Society shall vest in the Council for the time being, for the use, purposes, and benefit of the Society.

Executive Officers. 4. The Society shall be governed by a Council of twelve Members, to include a President, two Vice-Presidents, and an Honorary Treasurer, who shall annually retire from office, and three other Members (viz., those who have attended the fewest Meetings of the Council proportionately since their appointment) shall also retire annually, but shall be eligible for re-election, subject to Rule 13. Provided that if any sum of money be voted to the Society

Council. by Act of Parliament, or trusts conferred upon the Council by the Government, then it shall be lawful for the Chief Secretary for the time being to appoint, if he consider it expedient, any number of gentlemen, not exceeding three, to act as Members of the Council, and they shall have all the privileges as if otherwise duly elected.

Vacancy in Council, how supplied. 5. In case of a vacancy occurring by the death, resignation, or non-attendance of any Member of the Council for a period of two months, without leave of the Council, the remaining Members shall, in due course, appoint another Member of the Society to be a Member of the Council in the place and stead of the Member who shall so resign or absent himself; but such new Member shall be nominated at an ordinary meeting of the Council prior to the meeting at which he is elected.

6. In case of a vacancy occurring by the death or resig-nation of the President, Vice-President, or Hon. Treasurer, the Council may appoint from amongst themselves, or the other Members of the Society, a person to fill the vacancy so occurring, and the person elected shall hold office only until the next Annual Meeting; but shall be eligible for re-election for the subsequent year. Provided that such vacancy shall not be filled up unless seven days' notice in writing shall have been sent to each Member of the Council, stating the vacancies which it is proposed to fill up. *(Council to fill up Vacancies.)*

7. No person shall be eligible as a Member of Council unless he be a subscriber to the funds of the Society of at least one guinea per annum; and any Member of Council whose subscription shall be in arrear for three months after his subscription is payable, shall cease to be a Member of Council: Provided that this rule shall not apply to persons who may have become Life Members of the Society, by a payment of ten guineas, or who may be Honorary Members of the Society; and provided also, that a month's notice in writing shall be sent to the Member before his place can be filled up. *(Eligibility of Members of Council.)*

8. The Council shall meet at least once a month, three Members to form a quorum, and transact the business of the Society. *(Meetings of Council.)*

9. The Council shall have the sole management of the affairs of the society, and of the income and property thereof, for the uses, purposes, and benefit of the Society; and shall have the sole and exclusive right of appointing paid servants, as a Manager or Secretary, Collector, and such other officers, clerks, and labourers, and at such salaries as they may deem necessary, and of removing them if they shall think fit, and shall prescribe their respective duties. And such Council shall have power to consider and deter- *(Powers and Duties of Council.)*

mine all matters, either directly or indirectly affecting the interests of the Society, and if they shall think fit so to do, shall bring the same under the notice of the Members of the Society, at any general or special meeting; and to make such bye-laws as they may deem necessary for the efficient management of the affairs and the promotion of the objects of tho Society, and for the conduct of the business of the Council: Provided the same are not repugnant to these rules; to appoint one or more sub-committees, for any purpose contemplated by these rules; and generally to perform such acts as may be requisite to carry out the objects of the Society.

Branch Societies, &c. 10. The Society shall have power to associate itself with other Societies with similar objects, and to found Branch Societies.

Minutes of Proceedings. 11. Minutes shall be made in books kept for the purpose, of all proceedings at general and special meetings of the Members, and minutes shall also be made of the proceedings of the Council at their general and special meetings, and of the names of the Members attending the same, and such minutes shall be open to inspection by any Member of the Society at all reasonable times.

Moneys to be paid to Treasurer. 12. All subscriptions and other moneys received on account of the Society shall be paid to the Treasurer, or some person authorised by him in writing, who shall forthwith place the same in a bank, to be named by the Council, to the credit of the Society; and no sum shall be paid on account of the Society until the same shall have been ordered by the Council, and such order be duly entered in the book of the proceedings of the Council; and all cheques shall be signed by the Treasurer as such, and be countersigned by the President, or one of the Vice-Presidents, or by the Chairman of the meeting at which such payment is authorised.

13. An annual meeting shall be held in the month of Annual Meeting. February in each year, and the Council shall report their proceedings during the past year, and shall produce their accounts, duly audited, for publication; and the meeting shall elect by ballot the office-bearers for the ensuing year, and fill up any vacancy which may exist in the Council: Provided that no person shall hold the office of President or Vice-President, for two years successively.

14. The Council may, and upon receiving a requisition Special Meetings of Members. in writing, signed by twelve or more Members shall, convene a special meeting of the Members, to be held within fifteen days after the receipt of such requisition: Provided that such requisition, and the notices convening the meeting, shall specify the subject to be considered at such meeting, and that such subject only shall be discussed at such meeting.

15. The Council, or any general meeting of the Society, Honorary Members. may admit, as Honorary Members, any ladies or gentlemen who may have distinguished themselves in connexion with the objects of the Society, and at such meeting any other business of the Society shall be transacted, of which one day's previous notice shall have been given to the Secretary by any member desirous of bringing the same forward.

16. No Medal of the Society shall be awarded to any person except by the vote of at least seven Members of Council present at a Council Meeting, and after notice of motion for awarding such Medal shall have been given at the next preceding meeting of the Council.

17. It shall be lawful for any annual or special meeting Power to alter Rules. of the Society to alter, vary, or amend the rules; or to substitute another for any of the same; or to make any new rule which may be considered desirable; if and after

a notice specifying the nature of such alteration, variation, amendment, substitution, or new rule, shall have been given to the Secretary fifteen days before the holding of such meeting.   And such alteration, variation, amendment, substitution, or new rule shall be valid if carried by a majority of not less than two-thirds of the Members present at such meeting.

Zoological Gardens, Royal Park.

ANIMALS.

1 African Lion } *Felis Leo*
2 African Lioness }
1 Tiger—*Felis Tigris*
1 Panther—*Leopardus Varius*
1 Black Leopard—*Felis Nigra*
1 Leopard—*Felis Leopardus*
1 Hunting Leopard—*Felis Jubata*
1 Hyæna—*Hyæna Striata*
1 Yellow Fox—*Vulpes Flavescens*
2 Marsupial Wolves—*Thylacinus Cynocephalus*
2 Native Dogs—*Canis Dingo*
1 Silver-backed Jackal—*Canis Mesomelas*
2 Tasmanian Devils — *Sarcophilus Ursinus*
1 Chacma, or Ursine Baboon—*Cynocephalus Porcarius*
1 Papion—*Cynocephalus Sphinx*
23 Monkeys of different varieties
4 Native Cats—*Dasyurus Viverrinus*
1 Moongus—*Herpestes Griseus*
1 English Hedgehog—*Erinaceus Europæus*
1 American Black Bear — *Ursus Americanus*
1 Native Bear—*Phascolarctus Cinereus*
1 Blotched Genett—*Genetta Tigrina*
1 Racoon—*Procyon Lotor*
4 White Rats—*Mus Decumanus*
1 Tangalung—*Viverra Tangalunga*
2 Wombats — *Phascolomys Platyrhinus*
1 Porcupine Ant-eater — *Echidna Hystrix*

4 Zebus, or Brahmin Cattle—*Bos Indicus*
2 Alpacas—*Auchenia Pacos*
2 Large Kangaroos—*Macropus Giganteus*
3 Red Kangaroos—*Macropus Rufus*
2 Bennett's Kangaroo—*Halmaturus Bennetti*
2 Yellow-footed Rock Wallaby—*Petrogale Xanthopus*
4 Gloved Wallaby — *Halmaturus Manicatus*
3 Black Wallaby—*Halmaturus Ualabatus*
2 Paddymelon—*Halmaturus Billardiera*
2 Kangaroo Rats—*Bettongia Cuniculus*
4 Common Opossums—*Phalangista Vulpina*
2 Short-eared Opossums —*P. Canina*
2 Sooty Opossums—*P. Fuliginosa*
2 Small Flying Squirrels—*Belideus Breviceps*
4 Tortoises— *Testudo Stellata*
4 Barasingha Deer—*Cervus Duvaucelli*
2 Sambur Deer—*C. Aristotelis*
5 Japanese Deer—*C. Sika*
8 Formosan Deer—*C. Pseudaxis*
2 Fallow Deer—*C. Dama*
12 Hog Deer—*C. Porcinus*
8 Deer from Mauritius—*C. Rusa*

142

REPTILES.

1 Boa Constrictor
3 Tiger Snakes—*Hoplocephalus Curtus*
1 Large-scaled Snake —*Hoplocephalus Superbus*
1 Brown Snake—*Diemonnia Superciliosa*

2 Diamond Snakes—*Morelia Spilotes*
2 Carpet Snakes—*Morielia Variegata*
1 Iguana, or Coast Lizard—*Hydrosaurus Varius*
A number of Lizards

BIRDS.

20 Ring-necked Pheasants — *Phasianus Torquatus*
14 Japanese Green Pheasants—*P. Versicolor*
12 Golden Pheasants—*P. Pictus*
2 Copper Pheasants—*P. Sœmmeringhii*
2 Silver Pheasants—*P. Nycthemerus*
3 Emus — *Dromaius Novæ Hollandiæ*
5 White Cockatoos—*Cacatua Galerita*
6 Rose Cockatoos—*Plyctolophus Eos*
2 Corella—*Licmetis Tenuirostris*
2 Leadbeater's Cockatoo - - *Cacatua Leadbeaterii*
1 Solomon Island Cockatoo—*Cacatua Ophthalmica*
2 Red and Blue Macaws—*Ara Araganza*
3 Blue and Yellow Macaws—*A. Ararauna*
2 Green Festive Parrots—*Chrysotis Festivus*
50 Parrots of various kinds
6 Satin Bower Birds—*Ptilonorhynchus Holosericeus*
5 Bleeding-heart Doves — *Calœnas Luzonica*
3 Turtle Doves—*Turtur Auritus*
4 Native Companions—*Grus Australasianus*
1 Kagu—*Rhinochœtus Jubatus*
1 Horned Owl—*Bubo Bengalensis*
2 Chestnut-faced Owls—*Strix Castanops*
3 Australian Eagles—*Aquila Audax*
4 Hawks, different kinds
2 White Hawks—*Astur Novæ Hollandiæ*
   South Stone Plovers—*Ædicnemus Grallarius*

4 Weeka Rail, or Maori Hens—*Ocydromus Australis*
2 Ravens- *Corvus Corax*
3 Magpies, or Piping Crows—*Gymnorhina Leuconota*
1 Pacific Gull—*Larus Pacificus*
1 Kakapo—*Strigops Habroptilus*
3 Crowned Pigeons — *Goura Coronata*
2 Wonga Wonga Pigeons—*Leucosarcia Picata*
20 Doves of various kinds
20 Canaries
3 Native Turkeys—*Otis Australasianus*
2 Californian Quail—*Callipepla Californica*
3 White Swans—*Cygnus Olor*
2 Black Swans—*C. Atratus*
8 Cape Barren Geese—*Cereopsis Novæ Hollandiæ*
2 Toulouse Geese
4 Paradise Ducks—*Casarca Variegata*
2 Canadian Geese—*Bernicla Canadensis*
4 Maned Geese—*Bernicla Jubata*
8 Chinese Geese- *Anser Cygnoides*
2 Bar-headed Geese—*Anser Indicus*
2 Egyptian Geese — *Chenalopex Ægyptiaca*
3 Magpie Geese—*Anseranas Melanoleuca*
3 Mandarin Ducks—*Aix Galericulata*
4 Australian Black Ducks — *Anas Superciliosa*
2 Shieldrake, or Mountain Duck—*Casarca Tadornoides*
4 English Mallards—*Anas Boschas*
15 Indian Black Ducks

288

AT SIR SAMUEL WILSON'S ESTATE, MT. BUTE,
174 Angora Goats.

AT THE MESSRS. OFFICER'S STATION, MURRAY DOWNS, SWAN HILL,
19 Ostriches.

LIST OF DONORS

TO THE

𝔷oological and 𝔄cclimatisation 𝔖ociety,

1877-8.

~~~~~~~~~~~~~~~~~~~~~~~~

1877.

Date		Donation	Donor
Jan.	3—1	Wombat	S. H. Officer
	4—1	Diamond Snake	H. Green, London
	5—1	Black Swan	Mrs. R. Hoddle
	7—1	Sheep (3-legged)	John Gill
	7—1	Large-scaled Snake	R. Walker, M.L.A.
	13—2	Owls	Captain Phillips, *Frances Gertrude*
	15—1	Echidna	Miss Robertson, Carlton
Feb.	7—1	Brown Snake	Mr. Mackie, Kyneton
	8—1	Echidna	B. Cook, Brunswick
	8—2	Hawks	Mrs. F. Hepburn, Smeaton
	11—1	Native Companion	H. J. Gornally
	11—1	Echidna	Mr. Allcock, Hotham
	14—1	Diamond Snake	Mr. Davidson, Deniliquin
	14—2	Cape Barren Geese	Mr. Newberry
	19—2	Magpie Geese	Dr. King Ballarat
	19—1	Wallaby	E. Purton, Prahran
	21—1	Echidna	Jimmy Barker, Coranderrk
	22—1	Lizard	Mr. Swester, Hotham
March	2—1	Wallaby	Mr. Duncan, Coburg
	6—1	Platypus	R. Bushe
	7—1	Moongus	W. Moore Bell, Melbourne
	8—1	Wallaby	Master Duncan, Coburg
	14—1	pair Porphyrio Birds	Curcier and Adet, Melbourne
	20—2	Pigeon Gulls	Captain Stanley, Elsternwick
	29—2	Kangaroos	Mr. G. Rissley, Niemur
April	4—1	Monkey	Mrs. Fletcher, Carlton
	6—1	Opossum	W. R. Haig, Emerald Hill
	10—1	Echidna	Mr. M'Lean, Flemington
	12—1	Native Bear	Mr. Murdoch, Wangaratta
	12—1	Emu	Mr. Jew, Emerald Hill
	13—1	Monkey	A. B. Davis, Essendon
	22—1	Wallaby	Miss Landles, West Melbourne
	27—1	Lizard	W. Bowth, Hotham
May	9—1	Bustard	S. Clothier
	12—1	Opossum	W. Alexander
	14—1	Opossum	J. H. Bunney, St. Kilda
	25—1	Dingo	Hastings Cunningham & Co., Melbourne
	27—1	Leopard	His Excellency Sir William Gregory
	27—8	Ring Doves	R. Gibson, Royal Park
June	1—1	Owl	A. N. Smale, Hobart Town
	1—2	Native Companions and 1 Kangaroo	City of Sandhurst
	14—1	Tasmanian Echidna	H. Mitchell, Emerald Hill
	20—1	Luwack	G. G. Clarke, *Age* Office
July	4—1	Monkey	R. Gardiner
	6—1	Opossum	Miss Bath

1877.

July	10—1	Echidna	Norman Campbell
	14—6	Parrots	R. Gibson, Royal Park
	20—1	Turtle Dove	Miss Horton
	22—2	Fiji Parrots	T. B. Mathews, Hawthorn
	24—2	Francolins	Hon. S. J. Sumner, Stoney Park
Aug.	3—1	Grey Crow Shrike & 1 Plover	Dr. King, Ballarat
Oct.	27—1	Monkey	Robert Harper and Co., Melbourne
	28—1	Monkey	Colin Junner, Hotham
	28—1	Land Rail and 1 Owl	Miss E. Dick, Carlton
	28—1	Monkey	H. Stanley, Fitzroy
	29—1	Land Rail	Professor Johnson, Collins-street
	30—1	Genet	G. H. Gamble, Fitzroy
Nov.	4—1	Ring-tail Opossum	J. Halway, Brunswick
	7—1	Golden Pheasant	F. R. Kendall, Melbourne
	10—1	Eagle	Mr. Dyason, Echuca
	14—2	Native Companions	Shire Council, Kyneton
	20—1	Owl and Hawk	F. W. Thomas, Launceston
	23—1	Echidna	E. Arnold, Launceston
	24—1	Echidna	T. Harding, Inglewood
	26—1	Parrot	Mrs. Mahoney, South Yarra
	30—2	Parrots	F. Meaker, Royal Park
	30—1	Ring-tail Opossum	Colonel Hutton, Kew
	30—1	Rose-colored Cockatoo	William Smith, Carlton
Dec.	1—1	Echidna	T. Tidboald, Dargalong
	2—1	Bustard	W. Hebden, St. Kilda
	2—3	Pheasants	Hon. Niel Black, Kew
	3—1	Eagle	Dr. Youl, Melbourne
	3—1	Echidna	W. Stevenson, Brunswick
	3—1	Cockatoo	Mr. Bruce, South Yarra
	5—1	Echidna	Mr. Rudeman, Carlton
	9—1	Pheasant	M. J. Harper, Emerald Hill
	16—1	Dingo	J. Jillet, Broadmeadows
	19—3	Moari Hens	A. Loughrey, Richmond
	25—1	Kiwi	Captain Rowan, Melbourne
	28—2	Magpies, 2 Parrots	C. Meaker, Royal Park

1878.

Jan.	3—2	Molock Horridus	Mr. Sawers, Gawler Ranges
	6—1	Echidna	Miss Ferguson, Macedon
	14—3	Laughing Jackasses	Mr. Gibson, Royal Park
	15—1	Wild Duck and 1 Cape Barren Goose	Judge Bindon, St. Kilda
	18—1	pair Peafowl	J. Jacobs, St. Kilda
	19—1	Land Rail	D. Mort, Flemington
	19—1	Emu	G. Dill, Brighton
	19—2	Curlews	S. Young, Ararat
	19—1	Eagle	R. Washbourn, Tasmania
	24—4	Doves	Mrs. R. Dawbin, South Preston
	29—1	Porcupine	William Webb, *Age* Office
	31—1	Kangaroo	D. Mitchell, St. Kilda
Feb.	4—1	Hawk	R. Graves, Heidelberg
	6—1	Land Rail	William Kavell, Windsor
	6—2	Sleeping Lizards	Frank Godfrey, St. Kilda
	12—2	New Caledonia Pigeons	Dr. Duret, Albert Park
	12—1	Platypus	J. Hunter, Fitzroy
	17—1	Porcupine Anteater	Mr. Marshall, Eunemmering
March	3—1	Monkey	William Spence, West Melbourne
	3—1	Porcupine	C. J. Dulling, St. Kilda
	8—1	Owl	J. Gibson, Tasmania
	9—1	Platypus	Wm. Man, Latrobe-street E.
April	7—1	Native Bear	Mr. C. Tuck, Brighton, S.
	20—2	Alpacas	Mrs. Gellatly, Elcho, per favour of James Graves, Esq., M.L.A.
	25—1	Kangaroo	A. Jones, Carlton
May	5—1	Monkey	F. Baker, Emerald Hill
	7—4	Doves	Hon. Mrs. Bright, Mornington
	19—1	Owl	Wm. Crawford, Footscray
	20—1	Native Companion	Miss Chirnside, Werribee Park
June	2—1	Tortoise and 1 Albatross	Captain Pearce, barque *Irazu*
	2—2	Fruit Pigeons	F. Messner, Fitzroy
	4—1	Monkey	R. W. Hall, Fitzroy

STOCK ACQUIRED DURING THE YEAR 1877-8, BY PURCHASE, EXCHANGE, OR OTHERWISE.

1 Black Leopard—purchase
1 Boa Constrictor—exchange
1 Pair Canadian Geese—exchange
12 Californian Quail—purchase
8 Cockatoos—purchase
2 Carolina Ducks—exchange
2 Crown Gowra Pigeons—exchange
4 Dingoes—born in Gardens
1 Emu—born in Gardens
12 Fawns—born in Gardens

20 Golden Pheasants—reared in Gardens
3 Kangaroos—born in Gardens
1 Monkey—purchase
1 Ditto—born in Gardens
1 Mouse Deer—exchange
3 Turkey Bustards—exchange
1 White Hawk—exchange
3 Wallabys—born in Gardens
2 Zebu, or Brahmin Calves—born in Gardens

STOCK SOLD, PRESENTED, OR EXCHANGED, BY THE SOCIETY DURING THE YEAR 1877-8.

4 Formosan Deer—presented to Mr. W. J. Clarke, of Sunbury.
2 Monkeys—presented to Framlingham Aboriginal Station.
3 Japanese Pheasants—exchange.
12 Californian Quail—presented to Mr. Hinsby, of Kyneton.
2 Turkey Bustards—exchange.
2 Cape Barren Geese—exchange.
2 Shieldrake, or Mountain Duck—exchange.
18 Angora Bucks—sold.
1 Doe—sold.
2 Native Dogs—exchange.
2 Emus—exchange.
2 Maori Hens—presented to Captain Cooper, ship *Carlisle Castle.*

2 Emus
8 Cockatoos
2 Native Dogs
2 Eagles   } Exchanges with the Zoological Gardens of Batavia, per favour
1 Wallaby   of Captain de Hart, ss. *General Pel.*
1 Lion

4 Cockatoos
1 Wallaby
1 Kangaroo } Exchanges with Captain Elmslie, ship *Sobraon.*
2 Emus
2 Maori Hens

THE CALIFORNIAN SALMON

WITH AN ACCOUNT OF ITS

INTRODUCTION INTO VICTORIA

BY

SIR SAMUEL WILSON.

———✦———

PISCICULTURE.

It is only within a very recent period, that the science of
fish culture has become known, so as to be of practical use
for the multiplication of our food fishes, although the
keeping and feeding of fish in artificial ponds and basins
has long been practiced, and wealthy Roman citizens in
ancient times, did not consider their establishment complete
without their fish stews, to keep up a constant supply for
the table. According to Diodorus Siculus, fabulous returns
were realised from Lake Mœris, in Egypt, an artificial
fish-pond, constructed by the predecessor, of Sesostris.
Oysters were successfully cultivated in Lake Avernus, near
Naples, a reservoir since dried up by volcanic upheaval,
and afterwards at Lake Fusaro, where the industry has
been continued to the present day. The artificial care of
eels and other fish, has been pursued successfully near
Venice, at a lagoon about 140 miles in circumference,
called Comacchio, where very extensive works have been
constructed, and arrangements made, for the care of eels

c 2

from the time they leave the sea as tiny worms, till they are ready for market. But in all these instances there was no artificial fecundation of ova, and fish culture as now understood, was then practically unknown.

The first discovery of the possibility of the artificial impregnation of fish ova, was made in the fifteenth century, by a monk named Pinchon, the record of which was disinterred three centuries later, by the German naturalist Jacobi, who described accurately the method practised by Pinchon. But the subject does not seem to have then been taken up, and the discovery of Pinchon remained practically unknown, until in 1840, two fishermen named Remy and Gehin, in a valley of the Vosges, after years of patient watching and intelligent reasoning from the facts observed by them, at last discovered the secret, and found that the impregnation of the ovum took place after its exclusion from the ovaries, and when deposited in the gravel, and that the natural process could be imitated artificially, thus giving a certain and easy method, for the propagation and increase of any kind of river fish.

The story of the perseverence and patient endeavour, by which this discovery was made, has a strong element of romance. Concealing himself in the tall grass by the side of the stream, or in the overhanging branch of a tree by day, and by night when the full moon favoured his object; sustained against fatigue, cold and hunger, by that enthusiasm which has aided so many noble efforts, Remy desisted not from his pursuit, until he had wrested from Nature, the secret which had been so long withheld, and which was destined to confer a lasting benefit upon the human race.

It has often happened in scientific pursuits, that a discovery has been made simultaneously by two enquirers, who have arrived at the result by totally different methods. In 1848, the celebrated French naturalist M. De Quatrefages, on scientific grounds, brought before the Academy of Sciences at Paris, the subject of the artificial impregnation of fish ova; and in a paper read before that body, asserted the possibility by the artificial fecundation of the ova of fishes, of propagating them to any extent that might be desired. His statement was at first discredited, but the publication of his paper brought out the fact, that the process which he had advocated on theoretical grounds, had actually been reduced to practice by a poor fisherman of Bresse. The Academy appointed a committee to enquire into the matter, which found the facts to be as stated.

In 1843 Remy had addressed a letter to the Prefect of the Vosges, a portion of which the following is a translation, and is taken from a paper by Professor C. A. Joy, on fish culture : —

Joseph Remy, fisherman, of the Bresse, to M. the Prefect of the Vosges.

Sir,—I have the honor to inform you, that in consequence of the numerous experiments which I have made, I have succeeded after much care and trouble, in hatching an immense quantity of trout eggs, the young of which, healthy and well-formed, will be suitable for restocking the rivers. I deem it to be my duty to make known to you the means by which I have arrived at this fortunate result. . .

At the season of spawning in November, when the eggs appear at the vent of the trout, by passing the thumb and pressing gently against the vent of the female without doing her any injury, I cause the eggs to fall into a basin of water; after this I seize the male, and by operating in the same manner cause the milt to flow upon the eggs until they have become opaque. As soon as this operation is completed and the eggs have become clear, I dispose them between coarse grains of sand in the bottom of an iron box, pierced with a thousand holes. I placed one of these boxes in a spring of fresh water, the other in the River Bresse, in a spot where the current was only slight. Towards the middle of February the eggs in the spring commenced to hatch, while those in the river did not change until the 20th of March. . . . . In hatching the young, the tails of which first appear, are white, elongated, lean, with large heads. They move immediately, and appear, by their action, to swim with pleasure; every day they change colour, and assume the tints of the large fish; the body becomes round, and fills out. I have retained a quantity of these little creatures, in order to be able to reproduce them at pleasure. It appears to me that a discovery of this nature, especially at a time when the rivers are nearly deprived of fish, in consequence of the drought of last season, is worthy of the attention of the Government.

Signed   J. REMY.

Remy was awarded a bronze medal and 100 francs, by a local scientific body, for his discovery, which would have remained in obscurity but for the paper of M. De Quatrefages, which brought the matter before the whole scientific world. Remy and Gehin received a pension from the Government of 200 dollars per annum, and the former was granted a small monopoly in the sale of tobacco.

The question was warmly taken up by M. Coste, Professor of Embryology, at the College de France, who contributed greatly, by his labours and researches, to place the science of pisciculture in the position to which it has since attained. In England, the importance of the subject has also been warmly advocated by Mr. Frank Buckland, Mr. Francis, and some other ardent pisciculturists, and at Stormontfield, on the Tay, an extensive salmon rearing establishment has been erected. At Galway, the Messrs. Ashworth have stocked with salmon, some large rivers and lakes extremely well suited to this fish, but which they had been prevented, by a natural barrier, from reaching in their ascent from the sea. At Huningue in Alsace-Lorraine, a very extensive fish rearing establishment has been in existence for many years, from which hundreds of thousands of fish were distributed annually, to stock the French rivers and lakes. The work is still continued by the Government of Germany, into whose possession the establishment has fallen.

But the greatest triumph of pisciculture, is the successful transfer and acclimatisation of the salmon and trout, from the northern to the southern hemisphere, through the heat of the tropics. This has now been successfully accomplished by the aid of ice and steam ; the one to keep down the temperature, and thereby delay the hatching process, and the other to shorten the time required for transit.

In the United States of America also, great things have been done in fish culture by Livingstone Stone, Seth Green, Norris, Ainsworth and others, and several large establishments exist for fish cultivation. A fish commission has been appointed by the Government, of which the Hon. Spencer F. Baird is president, and with a liberality and generosity which does infinite credit to the Great Republic, they freely supply, not only for their own rivers —but also in hundreds of thousands—ova of the salmon, trout and coregonus, or whitefish, to stock the waters of Australia and New Zealand. The labours of the Commission have, in the States, resulted in a manifest increase of the fish supply in rivers where the produce had been rapidly diminishing, and the benefit which will follow their labours can not be easily estimated. In fish culture, the hatching of the fish is not the only difficulty that has to be overcome. In many places, high dams or waterfalls, prevent the fish from ascending the rivers to spawn. A contrivance called a *fish ladder*, has been invented, by which salmon or other sea-going migratory fish, could re-ascend the rivers. The fish ladder is simply a series of small pools, like steps of stairs, with an opening for the fish to get through, and a place where they can rest before ascending the next step. The invention has proved exceedingly useful, and it has enabled the owners of suitable waters, to stock many rivers and lakes with salmon, which were formerly inaccessible to migratory fish.

FISHING.

In Badham's "Ancient and Modern Fish Tattle," an amusing, quaint, learned and delightful book, there are many curious facts illustrative of the art of fishing. "Fish," he says, "being more distinguished for the size of their heads than for the amount of brains lodged in them, and affording an easier capture than either beasts or birds, fell early victims to the crafts and assaults of their arch-enemy, man;" and he goes on to quote early writers from Habakkuk and other sacred authorities down through Homeric stanzas and Oppians verses on the same subject. Suetonius speaks of gold and purple nets to charm the fish to a sweet death. History tells of Antony and Cleopatra's love for the sport, and how the latter played a cunningly devised trick off upon her admiring triumvir when he was unsuccessful in angling, by sending down a diver to fasten a fish upon his hook, which first delighted him with his apparent success, but afterwards caused him to feel annoyed with his inamorata for bringing him into ridicule.

From the earliest records down to the days of Isaac Walton and our own times, angling has been practised and enjoyed as being a most delightful sport. Sir Henry Wotton calls angling "an employment for his idle time, which was not then idly spent, for angling after tedious study was a rest to his mind, a cheerer of his spirits, a diverter of sadness, a calmer of unquiet thoughts, a moderator of passion, a procurer of contentedness, and begets habits of peace and patience in those who practise it." In ancient Rome the artificial fly was used as a bait, and fishhooks of hardened bronze and of steel were disinterred from the buried ruins of Pompeii. Martial refers to fish "decoyed and caught by fraudful flies," and Ælian describes the construction of the same by

"Around the hook a chosen fur to wind,
And on the back a speckled feather bind."

The same writer describes the art of angling as practised
in the river Astræus in Macedonia, by which a speckled
fish is caught by a fly made in imitation of the *hippurus*
a certain buzzing wasp-like insect of which these fish were
fond.   Arrian, in his history of India, tells of a nation of
ichthyophagi residing on the Persian Gulf, who not only
lived entirely on fish themselves, but even fed their cattle
upon it.   Their dress was made of fish skins, and their
huts were supported by beams and rafters, made from the
skeletons of the leviathans of the deep.   This wretched
people occupied a tract of country devoid of vegetation,
and being entirely dependent upon the fish they could
manage to catch, were in a constant state of hunger and
misery.

Thus fishing has been practised from a remote period
for the food supply obtained by it, and, as the calling of a
class of the population, but angling for the love of the
sport was the result of civilisation, and, as Badham says,
" was an afterthought not likely to occur till the world was
well peopled, and different states sufficiently prosperous
and advanced in civilisation, to spare supernumerary hands,
and allow the wealthier sons to follow less necessary arts
than the primary ones of war and tillage.   The Greeks
and Romans, civilised beyond the rest of the world, soon
became enthusiastic sportsmen."   The delight of salmon
fishing is so great to many for the health and amusement
which it affords, that although it is obtained by costly and
laborious exertion, the passion for it leads to an increasing
demand for the fishings at still higher rentals.   So much
so that the average cost of a salmon, taken by the rod on
the Tweed, is calculated at £3 to £5 each, although the
same fish could be bought in the market for one-fifth of

the money.   It is said by enthusiastic salmon-fishers that the delight experienced in the first tug of a salmon, when newly hooked, is a sensation more exquisite than any other sport can afford.   That the gentle craft is not more practised in this new continent, is partly from the cause that men are here all workers, who have little time to spare for pleasure or sport, and partly that our rivers do not contain the best kinds of sport-giving fish. As time advances and population increases, a leisure class will appear, and field sports, but especially angling, will, no doubt become a favorite amusement of a section of the population, during their holidays and times of recreation. Let us hope that when that time comes, our rivers may be plentifully stocked with those members of the finny tribe of the family of the *salmonidæ*, which are best calculated to give sport to the angler, as well as to please the fastidious palate of the epicure, when served on the tables of our prosperous citizens; and that these fish may become so abundant, as to be within the reach of every class of the community, and add materially to the food supply of our increasing population.

THE INTRODUCTION OF ENGLISH SALMON INTO THE SOUTHERN HEMISPHERE.

The introduction of the English salmon into the waters of Australasia has been frequently attempted, and many failures have been made, and much money spent, in the endeavour to accomplish this object.   No less than ten different shipments of ova of the *salmonidæ* have been sent from Britain to Australia and New Zealand.

The first attempt to send out salmon to Australia was made in the *Sarah Curling*, in February, 1860.   It was

superintended by Messrs. J. A. Youl and Edward Wilson,
and it was intended that the fish should be hatched out
on the voyage. Very complete arrangements had been
made to receive the salmon fry in Tasmania, by the Salmon
Commissioners appointed by the Government, and Baron
von (then Dr.) Mueller was entrusted with the care,
transhipment, and forwarding of them from Melbourne,
but this, like many subsequent attempts, resulted in a
complete failure, although some few fish hatched and were
carried alive into the tropics.

The second effort which was made to introduce the
salmon into Tasmanian waters, was a shipment by the
Beautiful Star, which sailed from London in March, 1862,
but the attempt was also a total failure.

In January, 1864, the first successful shipment was
made by the *Norfolk*: in January, 1866, that by the
Lincolnshire was also partially successful. In January,
1867, a shipment to New Zealand was made by the
Celestial Queen; also, in December, 1868, by the *Medora*;
in January, 1873, by the *Oberon*, and in January, 1875, by
the *Timaru*, from Glasgow. In January, 1876, by the
Durham, a joint shipment was sent to New Zealand and
Australia, which was partially successful in New Zealand;
and in January, 1878, by the *Chimborazo*, which was also a
partial success.

THE FIRST INTRODUCTION OF THE SALMON INTO AUSTRALIA.

The first successful attempt to introduce the salmon
into Australia, was made in the year 1864. A hundred
thousand salmon, and three thousand trout ova, were
shipped on board the *Norfolk*, packed in moss, in two

hundred boxes. The trout ova were collected by Mr. Frank Buckland and Mr. Francis, and the fish hatched from these are the parents of all the trout now in Australia and New Zealand, except those from the shipment lately received from England by the *Chimborazo*. The trout ova by the *Norfolk*, were taken from fish in Admiral Keppel's preserves in the Itchen, and sent as a present to Mr. Youl by Mr. Buckland. Mr. Francis also collected a lot of trout eggs for the same shipment.

The salmon ova were obtained by Mr. J. A. Youl, C.M.G., from the Severn, the Ribble, the Tyne, and the Tweed. To Mr. Youl is due the credit of the discovery of the proper mode of packing the ova for transmission on a long sea voyage, by placing them in moss and charcoal, in wooden boxes placed below the ice in an ice-house; and under his personal care and superintendence they were put on board the *Norfolk*. The boxes containing the ova were placed in an ice-house made to receive them, and were surrounded by 32 tons of ice. The ship sailed on the 21st of January, 1864, and the voyage occupied 77 days. The undertaking was a joint affair between the Victorian Government, represented by the Acclimatisation Society, and the Salmon Commissioners on behalf of the Government of Tasmania. The greater portion of the ova was forwarded to Tasmania, reaching Hobart Town on the 20th April. Arrangements had been made by the Salmon Commissioners, appointed by the Tasmanian Government, and a hatching apparatus was ready for the reception of the ova. On the boxes being opened, only one-third of the eggs were found to possess any vitality, and out of these only 3000 fish were hatched, notwith-standing that Mr. Ramsbottom, the son of the noted pisciculturist of that name, had charge of them, and gave them every care. The temperature of the water in which they were hatched was from 46 deg. to 49 deg. On the

pond in which the salmon fry were placed being examined,
it was found that a further loss had taken place, and the
number remaining was estimated at about 500 fish. After
a time it was thought desirable to liberate them, as the
period of their expected migration to the sea approached,
and those remaining, were allowed to find their way into
the River Plenty, about the end of the year 1865. These
were the first salmon introduced into Australasian waters.

A portion of the brown trout also were hatched out
successfully, producing 320 fish, many of which died;
about thirty were liberated in the Plenty, and only six
pairs reached maturity, and spawned in the ponds, and
the progeny of these have been distributed over many
rivers and streams in Tasmania, Victoria, and New
Zealand, and they are the progenitors of all the brown
trout in these colonies; but up to the present time,
it is understood that no salmon ova have been obtained,
although a few undoubted specimens of the *Salmo salar*,
have been caught at various times in the River Plenty.
A considerable number of salmonoids have also been
caught, which were supposed to be the true salmon, but
which appear to have been a species of sea trout, having
pink flesh, and which were caught of various weights up to
18 lbs. or 20 lbs. One of these was sent over to Melbourne, and on being scientifically examined by Professor
McCoy, was pronounced to be a fine specimen of the *Salmo
eriox*, a migratory species, of considerable commercial
value. The ova had doubtless been taken and sent by
mistake, with the salmon ova, the two fish having a strong
resemblance to each other. It was not intended that this
fish, which is commonly known as the " bull trout," should
have been introduced here, both the *Salmo salar* and
Salmo trutta being much superior fish. All doubts about
the *Salmo salar* having been successfully established in
Tasmania, have been set at rest by a specimen sent to

Melbourne in 1877, which Professor McCoy identified as a true salmon, although only of small size, being about four pounds in weight.

The small number of ova left in Melbourne—about 3000—out of the shipment by the *Durham*, produced a few hundred fry, many of which, however, disappeared mysteriously in the hatching boxes ; a small remnant of these were taken to the Upper Yarra, and 300 live salmon were stated to have been liberated successfully on that occasion, in a tank made to keep them for a time, of. which number about 120 were afterwards placed in the Badger Creek, a tributary of the Yarra, but up to this time none of these fish, or of their progeny have been caught, and there is no evidence to show that they have survived to propagate their species.

A second attempt was made to introduce the salmon into Tasmania, and another shipment of ova, was sent by the *Lincolnshire*, which arrived in Melbourne on May 1, 1866. The Government liberally granted the S.S. *Victoria* to convey the eggs to Tasmania, which was successfully accomplished by Commander Norman, under the superintendence of Mr. Ramsbottom. The hatching resulted in 6000 salmon and 1000 salmon trout. In Victoria, the acclimatisation of this fish was given up as being impossible of accomplishment, and the attempt was looked upon by many, as a useless expenditure of money ; as it was thought that the temperature of the rivers, was too high to suit the salmon, which is generally found in rivers which are partially frozen in the winter.

THE FIRST INTRODUCTION OF CALIFORNIAN SALMON OVA.

Having, in early life, obtained some knowledge of the great value of the salmon, in a commercial point of view as a food producer, as well as for the noble sport which it affords, I determined that another effort should be made, for its introduction into Australia, and, in 1874, Mr. Le Souef, the Honorary Secretary to the Victorian Acclimatisation Society, at my request, through Mr. Williamson, the Secretary of the Acclimatisation Society of San Francisco, ordered 25,000 ova of the Californian salmon. I had learned that this species was capable of withstanding much higher temperatures than the English salmon, and would probably suit the climate much better. The ova arrived in due course, but the supply of ice having failed on the voyage, the fish had hatched out, and, of course, perished for want of their natural element ; and on the box being opened, the ova were found to have become a putrid mass. Another shipment of 25,000 was asked for from Mr. Williamson, who wrote promising to forward them, but which, from some unexplained reason, never were sent.

THE SECOND IMPORTATION OF ENGLISH SALMON OVA INTO VICTORIA.

Up to the year 1875 there was no proof that the salmon had been established in Tasmania, although some enthusiasts declared that they were, without doubt, to be found in the Plenty River.

At that time, the Government of New Zealand had determined to attempt the introduction of the salmon into that colony, where the rivers and climate are exceedingly well adapted for this fish ; and, learning this intention, I offered to join in a shipment of 200,000 ova, one-half for Victoria. My proposal was agreed to, and, under the joint care of the celebrated naturalist, Mr. Frank Buckland, and Mr. Youl, C.M.G., both of whom are enthusiasts in pisciculture, a shipment was made by the *Durham* in the

year 1876, which arrived in Melbourne after a passage of
63 days. It was found, on examination, that about two-
thirds of the ova had perished, and owing to the unusually
hot season, the hatching proved a complete failure,
although ice was freely used. They were divided into four
lots, one of which was placed in hatching-boxes in the ice-
house at Melbourne; one at Geelong, under the care of the
Geelong Fish Acclimatising Society ; one at Ballarat,
under the care of Dr. Whitcombe, who undertook the
charge ; and one at Ercildoune. Out of the entire shipment landed in Melbourne only five fish were hatched,
which were from the lot sent to Ercildoune. The temperature of the water during the hatching was from 60
deg. to 65 deg., and although there was a large quantity of
ice used, the high temperature was undoubtedly the main
cause of the failure. In the moiety which went to New
Zealand, a more favourable result was obtained, and 1,500
fry were liberated in the Aparima River, being the produce
of this shipment. That greater success was attained in
New Zealand, was doubtless owing in a great measure to
the low temperature of the rivers there, the fish having
been hatched under a rill of water, at a temperature of
only 50 deg. Fahrenheit.

The enormous loss of ova in these shipments, appeared
to me to be owing in a great measure, to the eggs
having been shipped immediately after impregnation. It
is well known by pisciculturists, that in this stage, the
principle of life in the egg is most easily destroyed,
whereas, at a later period, when the embryo has reached
a further stage of development, the ova will bear
an amount of shaking and rough usage, that would
inevitably be fatal to them at an earlier period. To test
this point, I telegraphed to my London agents, Messrs.
Robert Brooks and Co., to have a few hundred ova
forwarded in the ice-house of the Peninsular and Oriental

Company's mail steamer; the ova to be obtained from the fish-rearing establishment at Stormontfield, on the Tay, and to be in the stage when the eyes are visible, as at this period they can be carried with the greatest safety. My telegram arrived too late, however, for that season.

THE SECOND INTRODUCTION OF CALIFORNIAN SALMON OVA.

This was very disheartening, but I still determined to persevere, and contemplated going myself to California, to superintend the packing and transit, so as to ensure a more successful result with another shipment; but seeing in the papers, that the New Zealand Government intended to import a large quantity of the Californian salmon ova, I applied to Mr. Firth, the President of the Auckland Acclimatisation Society, to order for me 50,000 ova for this colony, to come at the same time as those for New Zealand. He very courteously agreed to do so, and in due time, the shipment arrived by the Californian mail steamer, and was forwarded by Mr. Firth, with every care to Sydney, from which place they were forwarded by Mr. Barker, my agent, kindly assisted by Mr. Webster, and the ova arrived in Melbourne safely.

I will here give the account of the experiment, as it appeared in the *Argus* of November 26, 1877 :—

On the arrival of the ova at Sandridge they were removed, and taken by train and waggon, well packed on an elastic cushion of straw, and opened at the spring on Ercildoune estate, where the hatching-boxes were ready for their reception. On the pads covering the ice being taken off, a layer of moss, fresh and green as if newly gathered, was to be seen covering the ova. On this

D

being removed, the eggs were visible through the thin net-like web which covered them, and at once it was evident, to my great delight, that they were in splendid preservation, and far advanced in hatching, the eyes of the young fish being clearly visible.

The ova were packed in layers in a box or ice-chest, about three feet by four feet, and about two feet in depth. They were placed between two pieces of mosquito net, about seven thousand in each layer, and a layer of moss about two inches deep between each two layers, and also above and below the ova. Six inches of ice was placed over the eggs, and the bottom of the box was pierced with holes, to allow the escape of water from the melting ice. The ice was renewed every twelve hours on the voyage from Sydney to Melbourne. The box had an inner lining, enclosing about four inches of sawdust, to act as a non-conductor, and which answered the object sufficiently well.

The weak points in the packing were the use of cotton net, which rots and gets mouldy, while the moss remains green and fresh, and also that the ova were too closely packed together. For a short voyage this matters little, but in a long distance the difference is great, as when one egg loses vitality it soon decays, and the byssus, or fungus, which quickly forms, attacks all the ova within reach, which adhere to each other, and although little altered in appearance, these ova invariably perish in the hatching.

With little loss of time the ova were transferred to the gravel of the hatching-boxes, which had been prepared with great care, by being screened to ensure a uniform size, and by boiling, to destroy insect germs which might be injurious to the ova. All were got into the hatching-boxes the same evening, except one layer of about seven thousand, which were left under the ice until next morning. About 6 per cent. of dead eggs were taken out at once,

but many were adhering in clusters, most of which I knew
could not live, but which looked healthy enough at the
time.

The next morning over one hundred young salmon were
hatched, and they were lively little fellows even at that
early stage of their existence. When touched with a
feather they would start off and swim round in a circle,
and settle down again amongst the gravel. On the remainder of the ova being transferred to the hatching-boxes,
numbers of the young fish were found to have hatched
out during the night, and during the day four or five
hundred made their appearance.

The ovum of the Californian salmon is larger than that
of the British species. It measures almost exactly a third
of an inch in diameter. It is of a transparent pink colour,
and is nearly globular, being slightly · elongated. The
young fish is about an inch long, and it has attached to it
the umbilical sac containing the yolk of the egg, which is
of a clear transparent red colour, and seems quite as large
as the egg from which it has emerged. This sac contains
the food of the young salmon for three or four weeks, and
is gradually absorbed, becoming smaller as the young fish
grows.

The hatching process is effected simply by placing the
ova on a layer of gravel, over which a stream of water is
allowed to run. The temperature of the water is a most
important point, and I selected a spring from its being of
a uniform degree of cold, and from its freedom from sediment, which, by settling on the egg, interferes with the
supply of oxygen necessary for its vivification. As the
supply from the spring is limited, being only four to five
pints per minute, I had a pipe laid down from the creek
to supply two filters, the water from which is used to
increase the stream. The water from the pipe can be shut

off entirely when its temperature is too high, but for so far, the difference has not been great between the water from it and that of the spring. The temperature of the spring is 55 deg., and the pipe supply has risen on hot days to 62 deg., but the young fish did not seem to suffer in the slightest, and those in the warmest water are the furthest advanced. The hatching went on favorably, but a large number of the eggs arrived at a certain stage and failed to produce live fish. Sometimes after a struggle the head would appear, and the little creature would perish in the effort to emerge from the shell. In others, after the eyes were plainly visible, the living principle became extinguished, as shown by the ovum becoming white or opaque. The fish which were hatched, however, were strong and healthy. For a time the dead eggs picked out were over three thousand a day, and prospects were rather gloomy, but circumstances proved that it was more from the conditions to which the ova had been subjected before their arrival that the losses were attributable, than to their treatment after landing.

The total shipment was supposed to be 50,000 ova, but from a rough count the number received was estimated at 55,000. When the eggs were opened, one layer of about 7,000 ova was put in each box. The combined stream runs through the boxes from 1 to 8, the first boxes getting the fresh, cool water, and having the best chance, the water heating 2 deg. in passing through the boxes in hot weather. When the hatching was nearly finished, a very marked difference was observable in the number hatched in each box. No. 1 had only about 1,000 live fish out of 7,000 eggs. These eggs were on the top, nearest the ice. The next layer, in No. 2, had probably 3,000 fish out of 7,000 ova. No. 3 was the best of all, and there were probably 6,000 live fish out of 7,000 ova. Nos. 4, 5, and 6 were pretty equal, and hatched over 50 per cent. The eggs in No. 7 hatched out much earlier, but the percentage of loss was above the average. No. 8, opened a day later, and the lowest layer of eggs, hatched out very quickly, having the warmest water, and produced probably 5,000 fish.

It will thus be seen that the different lots of eggs, when treated exactly in the same way, varied very materially in the number hatched, showing that the causes of this difference were to be looked for in the treatment of the ova when first taken, or in the mode of packing, rather than in their management after their arrival in Australia.

After the young fish were fairly hatched but few losses occurred, probably not 50 in the whole number. Of the ova only about 500 remained to hatch on the 24th, and that day, although the hottest of the season, did not appear to injure the *alevins*, as the young fish at this stage are called. The number of live fish is now about 28,000, which is a not unsuccessful result. Had the ova arrived a week earlier probably three-fourths could have been saved. If they had been a week later, probably they would have been a mass of putrefaction from the fish hatching out, as happened with the first lot of 20,000 Californian ova which I had brought over three years ago.

Success, in most things, is the result of good arrangements, made with a thorough knowledge of the subject, and combined with favourable circumstances, where these are beyond control. The result in this case shows what a narrow line may lie between success and failure.

This shipment of ova had been obtained from the McLeod River, a tributary of the Sacramento, in Shasta county, California. They were obtained from the United States Fisheries Commission, of which the President is the Hon. Spencer F. Baird; and although my application was made with the condition that a proportion of the cost of

the shipment should be paid by me, the United States
Government, with a noble generosity worthy of all praise,
presented them free of charge ; a very handsome present
indeed, for which I made due acknowledgments on behalf
of the colony.   Mr. Firth, who interested himself in
forwarding them from New Zealand to Sydney, and who
incurred some items of expense, declined to furnish an
account of the same, although I am loth to cause him any
outlay ; and I would now thank him for his uncalled for
generosity, although I expected, and should have much
preferred, to have had the matter placed on a proper
business footing.

I had prepared myself for the undertaking, and obtained a good knowledge of fish culture, by reading
up all the books I could obtain on the subject, including the writings of Frank Buckland, Francis, Livingstone Stone, Norris, and also the papers on fish culture
which have been published in the proceedings of the
Societe d'Acclimatation of France.   I also gained much
practical knowledge, by having under my care, while
hatching, several lots of *Salmo fario* and *Salmo trutta*, and
was better able, after the experience thus obtained, to
undertake the care of the Californian salmon ova, during
their hatching and distribution in the Victorian rivers.

THE CALIFORNIAN SALMON.

The Californian salmon (*Salmo quinnat* of Richardson, or
Salmo lycaodon of Pallas) is, according to Gunther, of the
sub-class Teleostei, of the order Physostomi, of the family
of the Salmonidæ, and genus Oncorhynchus (Suckley
Ann. Lyc Nat. Hist. 1861, p. 312).

It belongs to the anadromous or migratory species of the salmonidæ. It is not intended to give here a scientific description of the fish ; it is distinguished from the Atlantic species, however, by having more than fourteen rays in the anal fin, while the *Salmo salar* has less than that number. This salmon is found on both the American and Asiatic shores of the Pacific (Gunther) ; a species believed to be identical with it, *S. Japonensis* having been found in Japanese waters (Pallas).

The name "*Quinnat*" is that given to this fish by the Indians, and it signifies "glittering," in reference to its silvery lustre. The name of a Welsh salmonoid "*Gwyniad*"—also in reference to the shining appearance of that fish—has a curious resemblance to the Indian word, and the coincidence is a problem for philologists to solve.

This salmonoid, similarly to the trout, salmon, salmon-trout, the grayling, and probably even the *Coregonus*, has, in its young state, the transverse bands or parr marks, clearly distinguishable, and they gradually disappear after a certain stage in the development of the fish—being a family feature of all the salmonidæ, in an early stage of their existence.

The quality which the *Salmo quinnat* possesses, and which makes it peculiarly suitable to our Australian streams and rivers, is its power of resisting high temperatures without danger, and even with apparent comfort. The habits of this species, differ somewhat from that of the *Salmo salar* in its period of spawning, the ova being deposited in summer and hatched out in the autumn, instead of being developed in winter and hatched in spring, as in the Atlantic species. In its native rivers the *Salmo quinnat* usually hatches out in October, after a period of incubation of about 60 days, at a temperature of 48 deg. to 50 deg. The time of hatching being extended or shortened, by a

lower or higher temperature, of the stream in which the
ova are placed.   It is an ascertained fact, that in ascending
the rivers for the purpose of depositing their spawn, the
fish have to pass through waters at a temperature of 76
deg., and as few of the Victorian rivers attain to higher
temperatures than that mentioned, there is a very strong
probability, that our streams will prove admirably suited
to this fish.   The average size of the Californian salmon
when full grown is about 20 lbs., but specimens have been
caught of 40 to 50 lbs. weight.   It is a handsome fish,
having a silvery lustre even at a very young stage, which
the *Salmo salar* does not attain, until it becomes a smolt.
It has not the elegant contour of the English salmon, and
the grain of the flesh is somewhat coarser, but it is quite
equal to it in quality and flavour, when in prime condition,
and the flesh is firm, sweet, rich, juicy, and high coloured.
It also gives good sport with the artificial fly, but the most
killing bait in fresh water is the salmon roe.   In its native
waters on the Sacramento river, a little snow falls occasionally near the sources, but the climate is mild and warm
in summer, and very similar to that of the seaward slopes
of our great dividing range in Gippsland, and near Cape
Otway.

The Californian salmon frequents bays and inlets, where
the water is deep, and spends most of its time in the
ocean.   There are no salmon in the rivers during the
winter months, from November to March, corresponding
to our May to September.

There are three ascents of this fish up the rivers each
year.   The first is in spring—corresponding to September
and October in our climate—when the largest fish go up
to spawn, which takes place at the head waters of the
streams, in the months corresponding to January and
February here.   The adult fish all die after spawning, so

far as has yet been observed. There is a second ascent of
fish in the season corresponding to February here, but the
fish are of inferior quality. The third run is of smaller
fish, in the corresponding month to April, being probably
the grilse going up to spawn the first time.

Enormous quantities of the *Salmo quinnat* are tinned,
and also preserved in casks with brine, by being simply
salted. It is stated that in 1875, 16,000,000 lbs. of tinned
salmon was prepared for exportation, on the Pacific coast
of the United States, besides a large quantity cured otherwise. If sold at the rate of 8d. per lb. this would yield
the enormous return of over £533,000, as the annual produce of only one branch of the preserving industry.

The fact here stated, that the Californian salmon is equal
in quality for the table, to the English variety, is contrary
to several statements that have been made to me. In
fact, one gentleman went so far as to say that he was sorry
that the Californian fish had been introduced at all, as it
was so much inferior for sport, and for the table, to the
English salmon. I have made careful enquiries on this
point, and the result has been quite satisfactory. Three
different gentlemen from Victoria who had good opportu-
nities of comparing the two, gave it as their opinion that
the Californian salmon was quite equal to the English
species.

It has also been maintained that the former will not rise
to the fly, but the information furnished by Dr. Hector, from
the reports of the United States Fisheries Commission,
from which I have obtained some of the facts mentioned,
expressly states that the Californian salmon gives good
sport with the artificial fly. I can at any time at my
salmon ponds, show anyone curious in the matter, how
readily they will rise to flies which are put on the surface
of the water. It is probable that an abundance of other

food, will prevent both salmon and trout from rising readily
to the fly, and until the rivers are well-stocked with fish,
fly-fishing may not prove very successful; but, whatever
the variety of salmon, it is likely that the habits and even
the flavour of the fish, will soon come to be what the climate,
food, and other circumstances will make them. It is a
known fact that in some of the Scottish rivers, certain
tributaries produce much finer trout than others; the
difference being so marked that an experienced fisherman
will, at a glance, tell the stream in which the fish has been
caught.

After this report was in type, I found in the January
number of the proceedings of the *Société d'Acclimatation*
for the year 1878, a short paper by M. Raveret-Wattel on
the Californian salmon, which gives some valuable information, a portion of which I have translated for insertion
here.   M. Raveret-Wattel states that :—

" Besides having well-marked specific characters the
Californian salmon is distinguished from the Atlantic
species by some differences in its habits, but above all by a
special aptitude for living in a much warmer climate.   We
know indeed that the *Salmo salar*—of which the abundance
in the North gradually diminishes as we go South, beginning say from 55 deg. of latitude—descends but little beyond
42 deg. ; which explains its absence from the waters of the
Mediterranean—the Straits of Gibraltar being about the
36th parallel—and also in America from the streams falling
into the Gulf of Mexico.

" The *Salmo quinnat* on the contrary is abundant about
35 deg. of latitude, and is found beyond 30 deg., which
gives good reason to think that it may be acclimatised in
the valley of the Mississippi. . . . . . .

"The Californian salmon will bear very great heat without
inconvenience.   In July and August it is seen in great

shoals on the San Joaquin, which river it ascends to a
length of about 100 miles through the warmest valley in
California ; where the temperature of the air, rarely below
75 deg. at noon, is often up to 104 deg. As to the water
of the river, it reaches sometimes 82 deg. at the surface,
and 80 deg. near the bottom. No other species of migratory salmon lives in latitudes so far South, as this one.
Mr. Redding of the Californian Fish Commission states
that in July and August when salmon are most abundant,
the mean temperature of the San Joaquin river is 79·7 deg.
During the same period the mean temperature of the
Sacramento calculated over ten years is 73·4 deg.

"A point equally important is, that this species does not
suffer although the water may be somewhat impure ; it
ascends the Sacramento and San Joaquin at the precise
time when the waters are most affected by the washing of
minerals, and seems to feel no inconvenience.

"The time of spawning of this salmon is prolonged
excessively, contrary to that of the *Salmo salar*, and seems
to last nearly six months of the year. It is known that the
time varies according to the locality, being earlier in proportion to the distance from the sea, and near the source
of the rivers. Thus in the upper waters of the Sacramento
the spawning takes place in the end of June or the beginning of July, thirty miles lower down the stream it is
observed to take place in July and August, and the farther
down the river, the later is the time of spawning. At the
junction of the McLeod river with the Sacramento, or
about 180 miles from the sea, it does not take place till the
end of August, or early in September ; lower still at
Tahama, the season is October and November. In some of
the streams which fall into the sea north of the Sacramento, such as the Eel River, and the Russian River, the
spawning takes place in winter, or in December, January,
and February.

"Not long since, all the tributaries of the Sacramento were visited every year, by prodigious numbers of salmon, which came there to spawn. The Pitt or Upper Sacramento, the American, the Feather, and the Little Sacramento had magnificent spawning beds; but since the extension of mining, the washing of minerals has nearly destroyed the spawning grounds of the American, and Feather Rivers.

"The Pitt and the Little Sacramento with their tributaries, have alone escaped this injurious effect of the gold-workings, and keep all their primitive wealth of fish-life. The spawning grounds of the McLeod River, an affluent of the Pitt, which has its source at Mount Shasta, are of considerable extent. It is to the banks of this river in the midst of Indian tribes ' of a doubtful sympathy for the pale faces,' that Dr. Livingston Stone goes every year during the month of August, to collect the eggs of the *Salmo quinnat* for the purpose of stocking other streams, and acclimatising this fish in other waters; the work being under the care of the Fish Commission of the United States. The distance from civilisation, and above all the presence of the Indians, have protected for so far, this region from the invasion of *prospectors* for gold.

"The waters of the rivers constantly fed by the melting snows are not troubled by the washing of minerals, and suit admirably for the salmon which literally crowd there in the spawning time. According to Livingston Stone it is not by thousands but by millions that he can collect the eggs, and although so many are taken to stock other waters, it has no appreciable effect on the number of the fish in the river.

"The ascent of salmon in the McLeod River commences in March, and lasts till October, some few arriving even in November; but when the rains of Winter commence, the salmon all disappear till the following Spring.

" In the principal branch of the Sacramento, the ascent takes place at a different time. The earliest salmon commence to ascend in November, and they increase in numbers till March. They are then very abundant and continue so till the beginning of June. During that and the following month the numbers diminish. In August they again increase, but diminish gradually till November, at which period they return to the sea ; just at the time when the younger salmon of about a year old commence their first ascent. There is also in this river in considerable numbers, a large trout commonly called the ' salmon trout ' of the Sacramento.

" The habits of the Californian salmon at the time of spawning, are in all respects similar to those of the ordinary salmon, but with the former the eggs are much less abundant. In specimens of equal size there is a difference of nearly one half in the number of eggs ; thus while in the *Salmo salar*, there are generally about as many thousands of eggs as the fish weighs in pounds, the *Salmo quinnat* only produces about 500 eggs to each pound weight of the fish. . . . . The time of incubation is about forty days, and in another month the umbilical sac is absorbed. The *alevins* are more lively and precocious than those of our salmon. At a year old they attain a length of 6 to 8 inches ; the second year they double in size, and at four years they often measure 24 inches in length. When full grown they may weigh 67 lbs., but 22 lbs. is about the average weight of the great part of those that are caught. They decrease in weight during the time they are in fresh water, and their appearance then alters greatly. They do not seem to take any nourishment while in fresh water. It is stated by Mr. Vincent Cooke of the Oregon Packing Company, that out of 98,000 salmon caught in the Columbia River in 1874, three only were found with some traces of food in their

stomachs, and these seemed to have quitted the salt-water
very recently.

" At the time when they leave the sea to ascend the
rivers, they scarcely differ from the Atlantic salmon, and
are beautiful fish with silvery scales, and of which the two
sexes differ little in appearance. Up till the month of
June they keep in good condition, and retain their delicious
flavour, which is exactly similar to that of the ordinary
salmon. But after this time they begin to get thinner,
become less elegant in form, lose the changing tints of their
coloration, and the scales appear larger and rougher.
As to the flesh it is already noticeably deteriorated in
quality. The nearer the spawning time the thinner they
become, their silvery lustre gives place to a deep olive
green colour and the scales become imbedded in the skin,
which gets thickened and spongy.

" The two sexes are then easily distinguished. The
females have their abdomens distended with ova; the
males, on the contrary, are thin and narrow; their heads
are long, and compressed laterally.

" They have, according to L. Stone, a somewhat ferocious
look, caused by the expression of the eyes, and the presence
in the jaws of formidable rows of enormous pointed teeth,
sometimes half an inch in length.

" As the season advances, these characters become more
marked up to the time of spawning, when both sexes
become so weak and emaciated that many of their number
die of exhaustion.

" On account of the length of many of the Californian
rivers, the salmon have to travel each year considerable
distances in their periodical migrations, and they must
often surmount numerous obstacles to reach their spawning grounds. In the McLeod River, the source of which is
3,500 feet above the sea, they have to ascend rapids for a

length of 30 miles. In the Snake River, the sources of
which are eastward of the Great Salt Lake, the journey
that they have to make is about 1,000 miles.

" In general, when they leave the sea to ascend the
rivers, they remain for some time in the brackish water
where the river joins the sea. The fishermen believe
that the change destroys the numerous parasites which
become attached to their body during their sojourn in the
sea. . . . . They soon, however, begin to ascend the
rivers, where they are immediately set upon without mercy,
by the whites at first, and afterwards, higher up in the
Indian territory, by the red-skins, who during a part of
the year live entirely on this fish.

" The *Salmo quinnat* can be caught very well with the
fly, like the trout or the ordinary salmon. Its own eggs
make also an excellent bait. But as salmon-fishing in
California is oftener followed as an industry than simply
for sport, it is principally by means of immense fixed nets
that they are caught, which completely stop the passage of
the fish at certain points known to be most frequented by
the salmon. This happens, for instance, near the limit of
the salt water in the Rio Vista and Oregon River, where
the quantity of fish caught is enormous. Extensive works
have been erected for preserving the salmon in tins, which
are afterwards exported to Europe, where they meet with
an advantageous outlet. In 1874, the preserving works on
the Columbia River preserved more than 22,000,000 lbs.
of salmon, in addition to the local consumption, which
might be estimated at 11,000,000 lbs. weight of fresh and
salt fish, which would make 33,000,000 lbs. of salmon, the
produce of one year from a single river, and since then
the numbers have increased.

" The works are on the bank of the river, upon which
are sometimes seen heaps of 1,200 to 1,500 fish. According

to the practice in Germany and Holland, they kill the salmon by giving it a blow on the head, instead of allowing it to expire when landed from the net. After having been washed in a basin prepared for the purpose, the fish are laid on immense tables, where workmen with large knives cut off the head with a single stroke. With a second cut they open it up in all its length, and then remove the entrails. In some establishments the head and other offal are not utilised, but in others they extract from them an oil of considerable value."

The paper then goes on to describe the process of preserving the salmon in tins, which is exactly similar to meat preserving as practised here, and states that:—

" In the fisheries of Oregon alone, this industry occupies not less than ten thousand workmen, and during the last season the exports, of preserved salmon have risen to a million sterling.

" We may ask if such destruction is not likely soon to ruin the fisheries. Already a remarkable diminution has taken place in the number of the salmon, and the Fish Commission has taken steps to prevent their wholesale destruction. Some fish-hatching establishments have been instituted to re-stock the different streams with salmon fry, to take the place of those netted for consumption. . . . . One of these, on a branch of the Columbia River, has an apparatus capable of hatching at one time 20,000,000 eggs."

From this it will be seen that energetic efforts are being made by the Government of the United States, to maintain in their rivers the supply of salmon, which from too close fishing has been diminishing for some years.

It would be interesting to know in what rivers the salmon are found as far south as 30 deg., as stated here by M. Wattel. Should the statement be correct, as to their

reaching so far south, the fact will have an important
bearing upou the question of the acclimatisation of the
Californian Salmon in rivers having high temperatures.

IS THE CALIFORNIAN SALMON SUITABLE TO THE MURRAY RIVER?

No attempt has yet been made to place any salmon in
the Murray River, but a few trout have been liberated
in one of its tributaries by the Acclimatisation Society.
It is not at all improbable that the Californian Salmon
would succeed very well there, if once established in sufficient numbers to bid defiance to the dangers of the annual
journey to the sea. The upper waters of this river and
its tributaries have splendid spawning grounds, and never-
failing streams of pure and cool water, which would be
admirably adapted either for this fish or the brown trout.

As the undertaking to establish the Californian Salmon in
the Murray and its tributaries would, if successful, benefit
in pretty equal proportions the three colonies of New South
Wales, Victoria, and South Australia, they might unite in
the undertaking, and contribute £1,000 each to stock this
splendid stream with, say, a million of salmon. It may be
said that the climate is too warm for this fish, but an
examination of the map will show that the mouth of the
Murray is in latitude 35½ deg., while its head waters and
southern tributaries are between 36 deg. and 37 deg., and
they reach altitudes of several thousand feet above the sea.
Let us now see where is the home of the *salmo quinnat*.
The mouth of the Sacramento is in latitude 37½ deg., or two
degrees farther north than the mouth of the Murray, and
the main course of the river is from the north, running
southerly, but its waters reach a temperature of over

E

76 deg. in summer, which is probably as high as that of
the Murray. The San Joaquin branch of the Sacramento
reaches south as far as to the 35th parallel, or half a degree
farther south than the mouth of the Murray. Seeing that
the brown trout has adapted itself so well to our high
temperatures, so much greater than any it could ever have
experienced in England, it is not unreasonable to suppose
that the Californian Salmon, which has been proved to be
so hardy in Victoria, should have sufficient adaptability to
circumstances, to enable it to live and thrive in a climate
and temperature so very nearly similar to that of its
native rivers.

Another danger to which the salmon would be liable
in the Murray, is the risk of being devoured by the
voracious Murray cod (*Oligorus Macquariensis*), but a
swift, active, and powerful fish like the salmon has little
to fear from a comparatively sluggish swimmer such as the
Murray cod, and it is even probable that the scale may be
turned the other way, and that the salmon might be well
able to hold its ground against the native fish of the
country.

The distance from the sea to the spawning-beds is
certainly great, but not farther, I believe, than the salmon
go in ascending some of the great American rivers.

I would strongly recommend that the three colonies
interested should take united action, and import five
hundred thousand or a million of the ova of this valuable
fish, to be placed in the head waters of the Murray and
its tributaries. Some suitable hatching ground could be
selected near Albury, in the Howqua or Delatite, or in
some stream high up in the mountains, where cool springs,
fed by melting snows, could be found, to provide admirable
hatching-rills, where the young fry could be nursed past
the dangerous stage of their existence. Should the three

colonies join in the proposed undertaking, and the experiment prove to be successful, each would derive a pretty equal share of the benefit. South Australia would have the fishing at the mouth of the Murray, where the salmon would be caught in the best condition, and Victoria and New South Wales would benefit pretty equally on each bank of the river; while the fishing in the Murrumbidgee on one side of the border would balance that in the Goulburn on the other. Should the Darling waters become stocked with this fish, the preponderance of advantages would rest with New South Wales.

If this proposal should be adopted no time should be lost, as from the present abundance of fish in the Sacramento river, ova can be procured in any quantity, and the United States Fisheries Commission are most ready and willing to share with other nations the immense advantages which they enjoy, in the abundance of fish of the best kinds with which their lakes and rivers are stocked. Should the fish soon become scarce, which is very probable, and the Fisheries Commission be obliged to retain all the ova procurable for increasing the supply in their own rivers, it is possible that great difficulty might be experienced in obtaining a large quantity of ova for a purpose of this kind.

But, it may be said, why not wait the result of the late experiment, and if the Californian salmon succeeds in Victorian rivers, ova can be obtained to stock the Murray, Murrumbidgee and Goulburn? To this argument I would reply that life is too short, the time to wait is too long, and that even should the Californian salmon prove as successful here as we could expect it to be, ova could not be obtained easier or at less cost, than they now can from California. The fact of this fish having been so very successful so far, is an assurance that the money to be expended in the proposed undertaking would not be thrown away.

In a recent number of *Nature*, a valuable scientific publication, Mr. George Francis, in a paper dated Adelaide, May 11th, 1878, states that the river Murray has this season been very low, and the water unusually warm. The stream running into Lake Alexandrina was very slight, the temperature of the water being 74 deg. The surface of the Lake on calm days rose to 76 deg., and the bottom temperature was 73 deg. In a stiff breeze the water stood at 72 deg. As these temperatures do not exceed those which are found in the waters of the Sacramento river, in all probability the Californian salmon would be well able to stand the heat of the waters of the Murray. Last summer was unusually dry and hot, and it is probable that the volume of the stream of the Murray had reached its minimum, and the temperature of the water its maximum, and that a more unfavourable time for testing it could scarcely be found. There is nothing in these temperatures to discourage the proposed experiment, but, on the contrary, they are not so high as those which the Californian salmon endures in its native waters ; and this fact is a strong argument in favour of the undertaking, which I would earnestly recommend to the favourable consideration of the Governments of the three colonies which are interested in the matter.

COLLECTING THE OVA.

The ova of salmon, trout, and of many other fish, when deposited in the natural gravel beds, in nests made by the fish, and which are called *redds,* can be collected and carried to a distance, to be used in stocking other waters. This is the plan adopted at Huningue, the great French fish-rearing establishment, which has now, however, changed owners, having been included in the territory ceded to Germany after the last war.

The ova when received at Huningue, is placed in artificial hatching beds, until the process of incubation has advanced to a certain stage, which is found by practical experience to be the safest time to subject the eggs to the rather rough usage to which they are sometimes liable, in being forwarded long distances. If they are roughly handled, or meet with any violent concussion at an early stage of the existence of the embryo, or immediately after the impregnation of the eggs, the vital principle is very easily extinguished. But when the hatching has proceeded till the embryo is clearly visible in the egg, they will bear being transported to long distances without injury. When the ova are about to be deposited in the natural way in the *redd*, the female fish excavates a hollow by fanning away the loose gravel with her tail fin. It is well known that divers can lift stones under water, in building submarine walls for piers, docks, &c., which they could not move on land, on account of their weight being less in water, by the weight of the bulk of water which they displace, and this principle enables the salmon to excavate their *redds* in loose gravel, in a strong current, with little difficulty.

The *redd* can be easily recognised by those familiar with its appearance, being simply a mound containing about a barrowful of gravel, thrown up into a little heap, with a hollow or furrow at the upper side, where the work was finished. When fish are spawning, it is no unusual thing for other fish of the same species to lie in wait, and devour the eggs in a wholesale way, and many of the ova are carried away by the current into deep water, where they cannot be hatched out and must perish. Many ova are never impregnated, and the enemies and dangers to which they are exposed, are legion. The water may become too low, and leave the eggs to perish ; floods may tear up the gravel and cover them over with mud ; frogs, lizards, water-rats, snakes, and numerous kinds of fish find a dish of ova a dainty feast. When the young salmonoid is hatched and reaches the *alevin* stage, it is equally exposed to perils of similar kinds, and at every stage from the ovum to the adult salmon, dangers encompass it and snares surround it. It is, therefore, easy to see what must be the advantages of protecting these delicate and helpless young creatures, at least until they are in a measure able to provide for their own safety.

The ova of salmon and trout, when deposited in the natural *redds*, can be collected by using a hoop-net, made of fine netting. This should be held in the current below the *redd*, while the gravel in which the eggs are imbedded is turned over with a spade. The gravel falls to the bottom immediately, but the ova, being lighter, float a little way with the current, and get caught in the net and can then be placed in damp moss, and taken to the hatching-boxes. It is not very safe to keep them long in still water, although they may be retained in this way for a short time. It is well to renew the water occasionally, or to have it aerated, to prevent injury to the ova.

But, as collecting the ova from the natural spawning-beds 'is attended with great difficulty, a plan has been adopted, of netting the fish when they are ready to spawn, and by careful manipulation, obtaining the ova from the female, and fertilising them with the seminal fluid, taken in the same way from the male. A little practical experience teaches the operator, to know when a female fish is ripe for spawning; the eggs having then left the ovaries, and descended into the abdomen, where they remain ready to flow out with a slight pressure, like shot from a shot-belt. The same operation is repeated with the male fish, and the milt is well stirred up with the ova, which at first are covered with a glutinous matter, which makes them adhere to each other. After standing for a little while they will separate easily, and are then ready to be placed in the hatching apparatus. The operation of taking the eggs, requires to be done with great care, so as not to injure the fish by rough usage. They are very difficult to hold, and if the gills be injured or the skin broken, it is almost certain to result in the death of the fish.

An apparatus has been described to me, invented, I think, by Mr. Howard, the curator of the New Zealand hatching establishment, which obviates to some extent the danger of hurting the fish in taking the ova. A sort of sloping stool is used, the top of which is about two feet six inches long and nine inches wide. To the lower side of this a small net is tacked. The fish is laid upon the stool, which is padded, and the net is brought over it, and fastened by hooks so that the fish cannot struggle much, or hurt itself. A shelf is fixed below, to support a pan so placed as to catch the ova, and by passing the fingers with a gentle pressure along the belly towards the vent, if the fish be ripe, the operation can be successfully accomplished in a few seconds, and the fish may then be returned to the water without injury. Where trout are kept in ponds, this method may be adopted successfully, and it is highly recommended by Mr. Howard, who has used it with success in New Zealand.

A plan has been invented in America, by which the ova of trout kept in artificial ponds, can be taken without catching or handling the fish, and thereby avoiding the losses which are unavoidable in manipulating them. The invention is called Ainsworth's Spawning Race, and it

has been patented in the United States. It consists of a
wooden box about two feet wide, and of the same depth,
in which wooden trays, having wire netting in the bottom,
are set, containing coarse gravel to allow the ova to fall
through easily. The box is placed in the bed of the
stream, where the water enters the pond in which the
trout are kept, and the water is made to flow over the
gravel with a rapid current, having a depth of 12 inches
at the lower end, and gradually getting shallower towards
the upper end, where the water enters the race. Beneath
the trays containing the gravel, a revolving belt on two
rollers is placed, with a handle above water, by turning
which, and by the action of two small bevel wheels, the
rollers and belt revolve. The boxes holding the gravel are
each two feet square, and the bottom is made of wire
netting of half-inch mesh. It is necessary that the fish
should not be able to get past the spawning race, or have
any other gravel beds to spawn in. The trays are filled
with coarse gravel, which the fish mistake for the natural
river bed, and the ova when deposited fall through, and are
caught on the revolving belt, which is made of fine wire
netting. A few turns of the handle bring the ova to one
end, where they are caught in a pan, placed there for the
purpose. If the race be covered, the ova may even be
taken while the fish are spawning, without disturbing them.
I have tried this race, but my fish did not spawn in it.
In the Botanical Gardens at Ballarat the spawning race
was more successful, however, and a quantity of ova was
obtained from some trout kept in a small pond, and which
ova were hatched out successfully. A full description of
this spawning race, illustrated with plates, will be found
in "Domesticated Trout," by Livingston Stone, a very
valuable work on fish culture. Another way of obtaining
ova from fish retained in artificial ponds, is by making a

race laid with suitable gravel, and after the fish have spawned, shutting them off by a screen and taking the ova, which may be done by lowering the water. This is the plan which has been very successfully adopted by the Tasmanian Salmon Commissioners, at the salmon ponds at New Norfolk.

The collecting of salmon eggs for shipment to Australia and New Zealand, is described by Frank Buckland, the celebrated pisciculturist, as one of the most difficult, and in fact dangerous, tasks that he has to undertake. It is at the coldest time of the year that the spawning takes place, and the necessary work when netting the rivers and manipulating the fish, with the thermometer below freezing point—sometimes up to the armpits in water—even if in a water-proof dress, is no easy or pleasant task, and requires an amount of enthusiasm in the cause of acclimatisation, and energy in carrying out the undertaking, that few men possess. To Mr. J. A. Youl, C.M.G., and to Mr. Buckland, the colonies owe a debt of gratitude for their exertions in the cause. To Mr. Youl is, I believe, due the honor of being the first to make the discovery, that the eggs of salmon and trout could be kept alive in ice, for a long enough period to enable them to reach the antipodes. And the first, and many subsequent shipments of salmon ova were collected and sent out by him, and under his personal care and supervision. Both he and Mr. Buckland have been unsparing in their labours, to achieve the desired object of stocking the waters of Australasia with the king of fish. By years of patient observation of facts, leading up to a final result, and hardships endured in packing boxes of ova in ice, with the thermometer far below freezing point, labours sustained by that enthusiasm which deadens the sense of pain, Mr. Youl did not even refrain, although his fingers

were numbed with cold, worn and bleeding by contact
with the sharp masses of ice, until his task was accomplished. Each new attempt finds these two brothers in
unity of purpose, *par nobile fratræ*, again with renewed
enthusiasm—often under very discouraging circumstances
—repeating their toilsome task.

FISH HATCHING.

We will suppose that the ova have been obtained, and
properly impregnated ; the hatching process next claims our
attention. The eggs must not be exposed to a dry
atmosphere, under penalty of their destruction. In still
water they will perish for want of the necessary supply of
oxygen, which all living things require to sustain the vital
principle. In moist air, or in a current of well ærated
water, the process of incubation will go on favourably.
Although salmon and trout eggs are usually hatched out
in a stream of water, this object can be attained equally
well in moist air, and if kept in moss, with a slight drip of
water to keep up the supply of moisture, and the temperature be not too high, they will hatch out equally well
without being put in water at all. It must be remembered,
however, that the moment they are hatched they become
fish, and like most other fish out of water, will die immediately if not restored to their natural element. As an
illustration of this fact, when the shipment of Californian
salmon ova which I received in 1877 was opened, it was
found that some of the eggs had hatched out some time
before, and that the fish had perished. Some had just
hatched and others were on the point of hatching, and
these were placed in a stream of water in the hatching

boxes, and they lived and will grow, I hope, to be 50-lb. salmon in the Gellibrand and Snowy Rivers, where they were liberated some time afterwards.

HATCHING FISH OVA IN MOIST AIR.

As the mode of hatching in moist air has not been tried, as far as I can learn, at any of the great fish-hatching establishments in Europe or America, there may be reasons which do not occur to me, which might hinder its success, but there are several advantages which the plan possesses, over that usually adopted. Those who have succeeded in hatching the eggs of any of the salmonidæ, will know that one of the great dangers to which the life of the embryo is exposed, is from the sediment which is deposited from the water—however pure it may seem—which is used in hatching. With a low temperature the time of incubation is lengthened, and this evil is then greater. Even filtering will not entirely prevent it, and where a strong current is used, no efficient filtering apparatus can be arranged to obviate this difficulty, which cannot arise under the moist air system. Another advantage of the latter plan is, that any injurious substance which may get into the water accidentally, and which might destroy the ova, could not affect them in air. The simplicity of the arrangements required for hatching in air is another great advantage, as compared with the elaborate apparatus required under the ordinary system, and a low temperature is much more easily maintained in an air-chamber, than with a stream of water.

The Californian ova above referred to, were, on their arrival, found to be packed in netting, in a box, between layers of moss, over which a few pieces of ice were placed, and the box had been kept in an ice-house with a uniform temperature of 32 deg. or 33 deg.   Of these ova 94 per cent. arrived in good condition, and over 50 per cent. hatched out successfully, the hatching commencing at once when they were placed in the water, and going on without interruption till all were hatched, the incubatory process having been almost completed in the moist air of the ice-chamber.

FISH HATCHING IN A CURRENT OF WATER.

The natural way in which the eggs of trout and salmon are hatched, is by the action of a current of water flowing over them, and the ova of the salmon, salmon-trout, sea-trout, as well as of all the other varieties of river and lake trout, are deposited by the parent fish in natural gravel beds, in shallow parts of the streams and rivers, where the current runs swiftly.   In cold latitudes, where the rivers are often frozen over in winter, the shallows having a rapid current are seldom frozen, and the constant supply of atmospheric air necessary, as well to the development of the ova, as to the existence of the fish, is kept up by the running water, which by rippling over the rapids gets ærated, and maintains the necessary supply of oxygen, obtained from its contact with the atmosphere, which is essential to the vivification of the ova.

It probably happens sometimes, that ova which are covered with gravel, may by the subsidence of the stream, be left above the level of the water ; and if the gravel in which they are imbedded continues sufficiently moist, these eggs may hatch out safely, and the *alevins* may reach the water immediately after being hatched ; but this must be a very exceptional case, and I cannot imagine such a delicate creature as a newly-hatched salmon, if buried in gravel, even to the depth of an inch or two, unless it be very coarse gravel, being able to find its way out.

The parent fishes, if of the migratory species, ascend from the sea into the same rivers in which they were reared, with almost unerring instinct. It being a very rare thing to find a salmon bred in one river, which has been found to ascend another river to spawn. Having found a suitable spawning place, which is generally sought for, at or near their place of birth, the female fish excavates a hollow by the motion of her tail, acting as a fan upon the gravel. It must be remembered that the weight of gravel in water, is very much less than on land, which renders this work comparatively easy. The stone, in fact, being by so much lighter and easier to move in water, as if the weight of its bulk of water were deducted from its weight in air. While the female salmon is excavating a hollow in the gravel, which is termed the redd, the male hovers about, and makes furious attacks upon any other male that may come near, and severe wounds are given and received, often leading to fatal results. When the redd or nest is partly formed, the female deposits her eggs in the hollow or trough which she has formed, and the male fish remains close alongside, quivering with excitement, and sheds his milt or spermatic fluid over the ova, which become fertilised by the process. The female covers up the ova by fanning the gravel over them in the direction of the current with her tail. This process is repeated day after day, until all the ova are deposited, the fishes retiring into some sheltered pool to rest after each effort. When the spawning is over, they become thin, poor, and unfit for food, and many of the males and some females, die of exhaustion. In fact it is asserted, that where salmon have to make very long and fatiguing journeys to deposit their spawn, as happens in some of the American rivers, that they are never known to return to the sea. When the period of spawning approaches, the male salmon has a cartilaginous excrescence on the point of his under jaw, which, like the antlers of the deer, grows with great rapidity at this time. This protuberance is common to nearly all the varieties of salmon and trout, but is developed to a much greater extent in the salmon, and especially in the *salmo quinnat*, or Californian salmon, found on the west coast of North America. The horny excrescence turns upward, and is sometimes several inches in length ; in some cases a corresponding hollow is formed in the upper jaw, the protuberance being occasionally developed to such an extent as to prevent the fish from feeding, which consequently dies of starvation. In the *salmo salar* it is less prominent, and still less so in the trout, and it gets partially absorbed after the spawning season, to re-appear again when the next spawning time returns.

The ova that have been deposited in the gravel of the river bed, or those that escape the dangers to which they are exposed, from their many natural enemies, remain for a period ranging from 50 to 130 days, before hatching. The period of incubation varies, according to the temperature of the water. It has been found that salmon or trout ova will hatch in about 50 days, in water at a temperature of 50 deg., every degree above or below this temperature, shortens or lengthens the time of incubation by five days. They would eventually hatch out, even if the water of the stream were at freezing point, but if once subjected to a temperature much below 32 deg., it is said that their vitality is destroyed.

The ova of the *salmo salar*, when from a ripe fish in the best condition, are almost exactly a quarter of an inch in diameter. They are perfectly globular, and of a transparent pink colour. That of the *salmo quinnat* or Californian salmon, is considerably larger, and is about three-tenths of an inch in diameter. They are very easily measured in this way. Take a board and place it in a sloping position, and lay a foot rule on its side, with the graduated edge on the side next the highest part of the board. Then place a few eggs above the rule on the board and cause them to run together, and then count the number which lie opposite three or four inches, and find the average number to the inch. One lot of English salmon ova that I measured, were exactly four to the inch, or a quarter of an inch in diameter. The eggs in another lot were nine to two inches, or two ninths of an inch in diameter, and the Californian salmon ova is almost exactly a third of an inch in diameter, being much larger than that of the English variety. The number of ova deposited by a female trout or salmon, is about 1000 to each pound weight of the fish. Different fish vary greatly in the number of ova, to the size or weight of the fish. Frank Buckland in his very valuable work on " Fish Hatching," gives the result of careful calculations of the number of eggs, which different kinds of fish are found to contain. A jack of 4¼lbs. weight had 42,840, a perch of ½lb. 20,592, a roach of ¾lb. 480,480, a brill of 4lbs. 239,775, a turbot of 8lbs. 385,200, and a cod of 20lbs. 4,872,000. From the enormous quantity of ova produced, it will be seen that if anything near these numbers were to come to maturity, both rivers and seas would become as Punch's Irishman said, "stiff wid' em," and as we do not find this redundancy of fish life, there must be an enormous waste or loss, of both ova and young fish. In fact the proportionate numbers of ova to the size of the fish, may be taken as an indication of the risk to be run by the fish, which an

actuary might calculate from these data. It has been estimated from close observation, that out of 1000 salmon ova
left to be hatched in the natural way, only one is allowed
to reach the marketable stage when the fish is fit for the
table, as a grilse, or an adult salmon. When a female
salmon or trout is spawning other trout and salmon lie
in wait, and devour the ova greedily. In fact ova are a
most killing bait, and their use is prohibited in England as
being unsportsmanlike. Eels, lizards, snakes, and birds
devour them; droughts and frosts may cause them to
perish, and when the young fry is hatched it is still more
liable to danger, as it is extremely helpless in its alevin
state. Notwithstanding all these perils, were it not for
the engines of destruction brought against them by man,
the rivers would swarm with salmon and trout, as has been
the case in former times in Scotland, and is still so in some
of the American rivers. If man has destroyed, however,
science has given him the means to replace, and where only
one in a thousand have come to maturity naturally, one in
five may do so with artificial hatching, and rearing to a
certain stage.

The mode of hatching salmon and trout now most
approved of, is to place the ova on fine gravel in shallow
boxes, and allow a brisk current to flow over them.
The dead ova must be removed, or they soon generate a
byssus or fungoid growth, which is fatal to any live ovum
which it touches. This fungus grows with such rapidity
that in a few hours it extends its thread-like arms, and
catches any living ovum within reach, inevitably causing
speedy destruction of the vital principle. Another
danger in hatching is the slimy deposit, which falls even
from the purest water, if not well filtered. The remedy
for this is a good filtering arrangement, and the use of a
garden watering pot to wash the ova with a brisk shower,

when any deposit becomes visible. The slime is injurious in preventing the proper supply of oxygen, required by the egg to vivify the embryo, from reaching it, and if the deposit be allowed to remain long on the ovum, it causes certain death to the embryo. The temperature of the water is an important point, and the coolest water is to be preferred, as fish hatched in cold water are said to be more robust, than those hatched at higher temperatures. A good spring, if not impregnated with any injurious mineral substance, is the best, as the temperature varies little, and the water is generally free from sediment. Any good water will do, however, even if muddy, provided some pure water can be used occasionally, to enable the attendant to see the ova, and by the very frequent use of the watering-pot to wash off the sediment. I have known trout ova hatched out very successfully by Mr. Richmond, at Learmonth, in water raised by a windmill from the lake, which was so muddy, that neither ova nor fish could be seen in it, until a few buckets of rain water were poured into the hatching boxes—which was done daily to make the ova or fish visible so that dead eggs or fish might be removed. These ova were within a few days of hatching, however, when placed there.

I will now describe the hatching boxes, which I have used with success, and which are very convenient, and in every way suitable. They are about six feet long by two broad, and six inches deep. They are made of three-quarter-inch pine-boards, and are covered outside with zinc with the joints soldered, so as to be water-tight. At the end is an overflow spout made of zinc, a foot in width, which conducts the water from one box to the other, and which, by being spread out in a thin sheet, gets aerated by being brought into contact with the atmospheric air. On the bottom of these boxes two or three inches of gravel is placed, so that the water

F

runs an inch in depth above the ova, which are distributed over the gravel. The gravel should be about the size of split peas ; if larger, the alevins bury themselves in it, and when they die cannot be seen, and when decaying will foul the water. If the gravel be smaller, when the watering-pot is used the shower drives it about too much, and buries the ova, and when any die they will produce the dangerous byssus, with the risk of injuring healthy eggs. A shallower box than that mentioned would suit the hatching better, as half an inch of gravel is sufficient—the object of using the gravel being to retain the ova in their places, and to keep them from drifting about with the current—too much motion being injurious to them. When the fish are hatched, however, more depth is required, as the young fish soon become lively, and may jump out of the hatching boxes, and a deep bed of gravel is useful to catch and cover particles of food, or the shells and *debris* of hatched eggs.

The hatching of salmon and trout ova, requires constant and extreme care and attention. Cleanliness is most important in everything connected with both the ova, and the young fish. Pure water is also of great import-ance, as a very slight thing may destroy a whole batch of eggs. In hatching English salmon, the lower the tempera-ture of the water during the period of incubation the stronger the young fish are likely to be, and 40 deg. to 45 deg. is said to be most suitable, but in no part of Aus-tralia, are the streams long at these temperatures. Even that of the springs rising at 2000 feet above the sea, being about 51 deg., and unless the ova can bear much higher temperatures than the authorities on the subject seem to think possible, there is little hope of the English salmon succeeding in our climate. The brown trout or *Salmo fario*, however, which in England is found in the same streams

with the salmon, bears the temperature of our streams
admirably, and the ova hatch out successfully at a temperature of 55 deg. to 60 deg. without any great loss.

The best place to select as a site for the artificial hatching
of these fish, is undoubtedly at a spring, where the temperature of the water is little influenced by atmospheric
changes. The water should be free from mineral taint,
and of considerable volume, so as to ensure a good
current. The ova are generally spawned at the time when
the temperature of the streams is at its minimum, and
it is therefore very desirable to have the command of
both spring and brook water, so that either or both can
be used if desired. When salmon ova have been brought
from England to the Southern Hemisphere, they arrive
before the end of summer, or about the 20th of March,
when the water still retains a high temperature, being the
effect of the solar rays, and unless a spring with a low
temperature be at command, the water may be found up to
65 deg. in a hot day, being high enough to make any chance
of success very doubtful. Even if ice be used, the difficulty
of keeping the temperature sufficiently low, both night and
day for a lengthened period, is found to hinder the success
of the experiment. The Californian salmon ova arrive
at a better time, or about the 20th November, and although
the summer has then set in, the water of the streams has
not yet been greatly raised in temperature, and the hatching out going on with great rapidity, the young fish
have made very considerable growth, before the great heat
of summer sets in. From this fish having different habits, and
spawning about the end of summer, the young fry are better
able to resist a high temperature, which, if injurious to the
ova in hatching, is certainly, up to a certain point, favourable to the growth of the young salmon.

It is a well-ascertained fact, that trout in cold streams

or ponds, do not grow at the same rate as those of the same age in warmer waters.

In hatching English fish, I should recommend that water be used of as low a temperature as can be procured, whether from spring or brook. With Californian salmon 60 deg. is not at all dangerous to the ova, but higher than this is probably unsafe; 55 deg. to 57 deg. I have found to answer well with them, and the fry will live in water having a brisk current up to 70 deg., or even to 75 deg. But a much lower temperature in dull, sluggish, running water would be dangerous, and the young fry have perished at once, when placed in water at 80 deg.

My hatching-apparatus was erected at a small spring, trickling down an oozy hollow, and rising out of the side of a volcanic hill. To collect the water and protect it from the sun, and from pollution by cattle, I formed a stone drain about three feet in depth down the channel, and collected the water in a small dam, which was filled with loose stones and turfed over. The water comes through the dam in a galvanised iron pipe, and is not exposed to the sun or to the open air until it reaches the hatching-boxes. It is perfectly pure and free from sediment. The temperature when I first tested it was constant for some months at 53 deg., which was a very suitable one for fish-hatching. From some unknown cause, which, as the spring rises from the side of an extinct crater, is probably the result of volcanic action, it has risen to 62 deg. in summer, or 60 deg. in winter, but the heat is now lessening. The supply is only five pints per minute in summer.

In the stream which runs close by, and which is supplied by numerous springs, a constant current runs at all times, and I have retained by dams, one above another, in its channel, the flood waters which would

otherwise run to waste, to keep up the supply in the dry
season.   The channel of the brook is a rocky glen
or 'gorge, and in some places the stream runs underneath large rocks, and into cavernous recesses, which lowers
the temperature of the water, even in very hot weather, most
remarkably.   I have found the water at the surface of the
dam 79 deg., and flowing over the sluice gate at this temperature, and it was reduced in a distance of 200 yards
lower down the glen, at the hatching-boxes, to 57 deg.   The
bottom temperature of the dam also, during all the early
part of the summer, keeps very low, being 55 deg. at five
feet beneath the surface, while the stream from springs
running into the dam was 80 deg., and the surface stratum
of water in it of the same temperature.   On making the
discovery that there was this difference of 25 deg. between
the top and bottom temperature, I arranged so as to
draw off the water from the bottom of the dam, instead of
allowing it to overflow at the sluice-gate, and thus, by
maintaining a lower temperature in the hatching-boxes,
contributed greatly to the success of my undertaking.

The water of this stream is dammed up by a little stone
and cement work under a rock, and carried by a two-inch
galvanised iron pipe, which is covered with a hay-rope wound
round it to protect it from the sun and to keep down the
temperature.   The hatching-boxes are seven in number,
and in addition to them, I had a stone and cement race
constructed on the ground, divided down the centre, and so
arranged that the water would circulate with a gentle
current through all the boxes, up one side of the race
and down the other ; there are little miniature waterfalls
from one box to another, to aerate the water, which
finally flows through four small ponds, fitted with gratings
to retain the young fish, when they are sufficiently
advanced to require this precaution, and covered with

netting to keep off shags and cormorants. The water of
the brook being muddy, I had a very elaborate filtering
arrangement erected, which, however, was of little service,
as it filtered but a small quantity of water, and I found it
better, as the hatching was going on rapidly, to dispense
with filtering and make use of a larger stream.   The
hatching-boxes are at different levels, beginning at four
feet above the ground, and going down to two feet, a fall
being required from one to the other.   Each box is set
perfectly level, and the current is regulated by the depth
of gravel.   •

Many experiments as to the best mode of fish-hatching
have been tried, and a very efficient apparatus has been
invented by M. Coste, the great French Pisciculturist,
consisting of a zinc or iron japanned trough, having
movable frames fitted with glass rods, between which
the ova lie suspended, allowing any sediment or particles
of hatched eggs to fall through, and which may be cleaned
out without disturbing the eggs.   This hatching-box
obviates the difficulty that has been experienced, of a
fungoid growth which is apt to form on wooden hatching-
boxes, but it is more suited for an amateur to hatch out a
few ova, than for hatching large numbers.

An American discovery, of the advantages to be obtained
by the use of charred wood for hatching-boxes, has solved
the problem most satisfactorily, it having been found that
no fungus appeared on the carbonaceous surface, after a
long and severe test.   In one of the hatching-boxes, by
way of experiment, I placed a bottom of ribbed glass,
but found, after trying this and also a charcoal bed,
that nothing suited so well as fine gravel, of a dark
colour.   If the gravel be of a light colour, the dead eggs
are less easily seen, from their colour being also white.
It is better that the hatching-boxes should be three to

four feet above the ground, for convenience in picking out the dead eggs, and for examination of the fish and eggs from time to time. The stone race being on the level of the ground necessitates the kneeling posture in examining them, which becomes very irksome and inconvenient, as the young fish cannot be seen so well, and dead ones may be left in the race, thereby fouling the water, to the injury of the live fish.

The hatching-boxes were each secured at the ends with fine screens of perforated tin. These must be smaller in the perforations than the finest perforated zinc that I could obtain, which I found would let young fish go through. I first tried woven screens of copper wire, but finding the deaths amongst the ova to increase rapidly, I suspected that something was wrong, and had tin ones inserted instead. I found that I had unwittingly, by the combination of zinc and copper, constructed a galvanic battery, which, no doubt, was destroying the ova. I found that M. Coste had on one occasion made the same mistake, which he described in a paper sent to the *Societé Imperiale d'Acclimatation*, and which suggested this as the possible cause of the loss which had occurred. The boxes were also divided by a screen into two parts, to prevent the young fish from crowding to the end where the water enters, which they are eager to do.

The boxes must be kept carefully covered, so that not a crevice may be left where a mouse, snake, or lizard could enter, as they would make short work of either ova or *alevins*—as the newly-hatched fish, until the umbilical sac is absorbed, are called—once they gained access to them. A portion of the cover should be of perforated zinc, to admit light, which, although not needed during the process of hatching, is essential to the health of the young fish when hatched.

The boxes being all in their places, and the water running
well from one to the other throughout, and the screens
fitted in their slides, the gravel may be put in them.
It should be well washed, and, if river gravel, it
should be boiled, so as to kill any eggs of water insects
that it may contain.   It must first be carefully screened
to the right size, one screen taking out the larger gravel,
and another the sand and fine gravel.   When it is
ready it must be spread smoothly and evenly over the
bottom, to such a depth as will leave from half an inch
to an inch of water over it, according to the supply.   The
current should be brisk, but not strong enough to carry
about the eggs, as rest is essential to the development of
the embryo.   When the gravel has been put in the boxes,
they are then ready to receive the ova.   If these have
been packed in snow or ice, they should not be at once
placed in water that may be much warmer, but the water
should be brought down to say 40 deg. by the use of ice,
or some other means of preventing the injurious effects
of the shock caused by a sudden change of temperature.
Then the ova may be distributed equally in the boxes,
and a small stream of water turned on, to bring up the
temperature by degrees, to that of the water in which they
are to be hatched.   It is very dangerous to expose the ova
to dry air of a high temperature, and they should be placed
in the hatching-boxes moss and all, and the moss can be
easily picked out afterwards.   Care must be taken not to
keep them for any great length of time in still water,
as it is likely to kill the embryo, and where water is
abundant, a good current should be maintained.   A
stream of fifteen or twenty pints per minute would serve
to hatch 50,000 ova, with an occasional shower from
the watering-pot, and the water should be made to
fall some distance, or be forced through a small aperture

under pressure, to ærate it thoroughly. With a stream of four or five pints per minute 1000 ova may be hatched, or even two or three times that number. But much depends on constant care and attention to minute details, which readily suggest themselves to the attendant. The moss having been removed, and any foreign substance, the attendant should use a feather from a goose or turkey's wing, and a pair of pincers made out of wire, about the size of knitting-needles, with the ends turned in a circle with the opening about the size to hold an egg, to pick out dead eggs. The ova should be distributed evenly over the gravel by using the feather. A little practice will enable this to be done without touching the eggs, simply by causing a current over them, and as they are but little heavier than water, they are easily moved about in it. One thousand eggs can be hatched to the square foot of space in the hatching-boxes, but double this space is better, and after the fish are hatched, much more room and an increased current of water, is required to do them justice.

In a new fish-hatching institution lately established by Livingston Stone, a mode of hatching was adopted with success, which greatly economises space in the hatching-race. The eggs were placed five or six layers deep in baskets made of galvanized wire, and the current was made to rise up through them from below. The baskets were placed across the current in the hatching-race, and no gravel whatever was used. When hatching was about to commence, the ova were removed to a hatching-race, where they had sufficient room to ensure their proper development. This plan was adopted to enable Mr. Stone to hatch out a large number of eggs which he had obtained, but had not been able to get proper appliances made in time, to hatch them in the ordinary way. The establishment is on a branch of the Columbia river, in the Oregon

territory, where the fisheries had been found to be getting
less productive.

When a white speck, however small, appears in an egg,
it is a sign that the embryo within will die, and speedily
the whole egg becomes white and opaque.   Dead eggs
must be removed as soon as possible, as, if this be not
done, the fatal byssus soon appears, and if not removed it
spreads from egg to egg, destroying all it touches.

The healthy impregnated ovum of the salmon is of a
deep pink colour, and consists of a horny outer shell,
which is filled principally with a semi-transparent viscous
fluid, resembling the albumen of a hen's egg, in which may
be seen floating the yolk, of a pink colour, and some oil
globules of a deeper pink.   On closely examining the egg
against the light a spot is visible, resembling a light seen
through a fog, and this is the embryo of the fish within.
After a time a white line appears dimly, curved round
inside of the shell, which is the outline of the fish; the
bright spot soon becomes more definite in outline, and a faint
dot appears, which is the eye of the fish.   After a few
days the head and both eyes may be seen dimly, and the
egg may be seen to roll about in the current, without
apparent cause.   At this stage the ova will bear transport
better than at any other time, but it is most difficult to
do so with safety during the earlier stages of the incubatory
process.   The knowledge of this fact is of great importance
to those engaged in pisciculture.

After the eyes of the young fish are plainly visible, only
a few days will elapse before some of the ova will be
hatched out.   If the egg be examined at this stage against
a strong light, by looking through it the movements of the
embryo, can be plainly seen inside the semi-transparent
shell.   At last the interesting process, of the development
of a living fish, from a minute germinal spot floating in

albumen, is completed; the young fish becomes too
large for its prison, and the shell bursts open, liberating
the captive. Where there are many ova hatching out, the
observer may be fortunate enough, to see this very interesting phenomenon take place before his eyes. Sometimes
the head comes out first, and the shell adheres to the sac
for a time, till a last grand effort frees the young *alevin*
which lies panting with the exertion, and the novelty of its
position, exercising vigorously its lungs, or the breathing
apparatus in its gills, which performs the same office.

At first a few fish will hatch out during two or three
days, and then the great bulk of them will come, the whole
being hatched in about ten or twelve days, and some
unimpregnated ova in which no fish exist will remain good
and sound to the last.

During the time of hatching, the watering-pot should
be used freely, and indeed all through the time of incubation, when sediment becomes troublesome. When the
hatching is going on, the empty shells and *debris* of the
eggs, are by it washed away and get collected against the
screens, when they can be removed. The current of water
should now be increased a little, and a slightly higher
temperature is not objectionable. The *alevin* stage of the
fish, is the least troublesome time in the rearing of young
trout or salmon. They do not require any food, and are
little liable to loss at this period. A little very fine earthy
gravel, should be spread over the coarser gravel in the
hatching boxes, to cover up and deodorise any particles of
decaying eggs which may be in the gravel. Of course all
dead fish should be removed at once, as decay sets in very
speedily. Every second day, a sprinkling of fine volcanic
earth, or good loam not of an adhesive nature, is very bene-
ficial, and it should be scattered over the surface of the
water. The shower should be used two or three times

daily, and everything should be kept scrupulously clean. The *alevins* collect in clusters, in corners sheltered from the current, and lie on their sides closely packed together, like herrings in a barrel, sometimes taking a start and going about for a foot or two.

The appearance of the newly-hatched fish, is not the least like that of a salmon. There appears a mass of transparent pink gum, with a thin body attached to it about three-quarters of an inch in length. This is the body of the fish, and the large, shapeless head, and enormous goggle eyes, are very remarkable; the dorsal, or back fin, seems to extend the whole way from the head to the tail. The body and umbilical appendage, seem larger than the egg they have just emerged from. The sac is elongated and tapers slightly, and contains the food required by the fish during its *alevin* stage. As the *alevin* grows, the sac gradually diminishes, until it is quite absorbed. At this stage the fish is perfectly formed, the continuous back fin, having divided into the dorsal, adipose, and caudal fins, and the body has become developed in proportion to the head, into a perfectly-formed and shapely fish.

When the umbilical sac is absorbed, the young salmon is called a parr, and already the transverse bars may be seen on the sides of the fish, which continue to distinguish the parr, until it reaches the smolt stage. These bars are common to most, if not all the varieties of trout and salmon, which are very similar in appearance at this early stage, and they are then most difficult to distinguish from each other. The migratory species however, have a larger number of bars than the non-migratory.

Although the *alevins* do not require much, or any food, until the umbilical sac is absorbed, it is wise to begin to offer them some a little before that stage is reached by the earliest hatched amongst them. Otherwise, should

they get ravenously hungry before food is offered, some
may get too weak, and perish without being able to
partake of the unaccustomed food, or they may gorge
themselves, causing illness, heavy losses being the result.
The food which it is most convenient to use, and which
answers exceedingly well, is the liver of sheep or other
animals, boiled and grated on a nutmeg-grater, then
rubbed into the consistency of cream with a little water,
by the use of a table-knife on a board. In this way
the particles are made fine enough, so as not to choke
the young fish. The meat must be perfectly fresh, and
should be prepared frequently, and care should be taken,
that not too much is given at a time, as it decays very
speedily, and will foul the water. Other food is recommended by some, such as eggs, soured milk, and the
minute roe of sea fish; but liver is easily obtained, and is
on the whole, more convenient than any other food.

Earth should be used at least every second day, a little
being sprinkled all over the hatching-box, and the fish will
be found to disperse themselves over every inch of the
box, hunting about for something that they find in it, and
seeming to enjoy it greatly. It probably contains micros-
copic insects invisible to the unaided human eye. Whether
it be the variety of food obtained from the earth, or some
mineral constituent in it that they require, certain it is
that the use of earth is a most important part of their
treatment. It also acts as a deodoriser and purifier of
any decaying or fæcal matter which may be in the gravel.

The shower should also be continued two or three times
daily, and two or three small sods with the grass on them,
are useful to supply a little vegetable diet. The food
should be given three or four times a day at first, in very
small quantities, and care should be taken that little or
none is wasted, as it is dangerous when decaying, causing
the water to become putrid.

It is stated that a fish eats one-hundredth part of his weight daily, and this rule may give some indication of the quantity of food to be given. If too much is put in the water, by its decay it becomes a great source of danger to the fish.

THE LIBERATION OF YOUNG FISH.

Just before the *alevins* lose their sacs, and while they require but little food, is a good time to transport them, especially where the distance to their destination is great. At this stage they are much more easily carried, than when they grow to a considerably larger size, and many think that by being early accustomed to face danger, they are more likely to come successfully through the perils they have to encounter, than if trained to come for their food, and partially domesticated, without having any knowledge of the dangers that they must encounter when liberated in the open waters. Where salmon can be retained in ponds until they attain the smolt stage, and put on their silvery coat, preparatory to commencing their migration to the sea, and where every care is taken of them, it would, no doubt, be more in their favour, and a larger number would probably survive, than if they had been exposed to all the perils of the river; but if they had to be transported to a distance before being liberated, the risk of loss with fish of the size that they would then attain to, would more than counterbalance the loss from their early liberation.

THE TRANSPORT OF LIVE FISH.

The transport of live fish to long distances has been a most difficult problem, until it was discovered that the main want of the fish was atmospheric air, or the oxygen contained in it. It may seem strange at first sight, that fish should need air when they always live in the water, and still more so that they cannot rise to the surface, and obtain the needed oxygen from the air that is so easily within their reach. It is found in practice, however, that few river fish will live long in a vessel of still water, unless there be a current running into it. It is true that pond fish can do so, but they have the faculty of sucking in air at the surface of the water, as may often be seen in the glass globes, in which the golden carp are usually kept.

An interesting experiment is detailed in "Land and Water," in which a number of adult specimens of salmon, perch, black bass, &c., were conveyed from the Atlantic to the Pacific Ocean, or from New York to California.

The fish were carried in a waggon fitted up expressly for the purpose, and belonging to the United States Fish Commission. Round the waggon are ranged tanks to hold the fish, of a convenient size for moving about in transit. Each has a siphon of indiarubber, to allow the water to be drawn off and renewed, when necessary, without disturbing the fish.

A special arrangement provides for ærating the water during the journey. On one of the axles of the waggon is fixed a wheel, which, by means of an endless belt, drives an air-pump, which is worked constantly while the train is in motion. The air is forced into an indiarubber tube having a branch to each tank, each branch being fitted with a stop-cock, to regulate the supply of air. By the aid of this ingenious arrangement, more than 150 breeding fish of nine varieties, were carried without serious loss across the American continent. For the sea-fish, a supply of sea-water was sent from California to meet them, to renew the water on the journey, and which was found of great service.

In China, live fish are carried to market on barges and boats, down the rivers and canals, in tanks into which a constant shower of water is allowed to fall, from a bamboo pierced with holes, and connected with another tank, which is replenished from time to time. The water, by being brought into contact with the air, gets aerated, and so keeps the fish supplied with oxygen, and in a healthy state. An eye witness was surprised to find, that after the great care that was taken of the fish on the journey, when they reached their destination they were taken out of the water, and pitched into a boat in the most careless way, to be carried off to the market for sale.

The great secret of success in transporting live fish safely, is to keep the temperature of the water in which they are carried, at the same temperature to which they have been accustomed, by using ice if necessary; and to have the water constantly and thoroughly aerated, by forcing air into it with bellows and an indiarubber tube. For all the varieties of salmon and trout, a low temperature in transit is much safer than a comparatively high one. At 50 deg. to 55 deg. the risk is little, if other important matters be carefully attended to. In the winter season, and with small numbers, it is comparatively easy to transport them to any reasonable distance, but in summer the risk is enormously increased.

The plan that I adopted with great success, was to put the fish in cans, resembling the milk cans used by dairymen for carrying their milk. A perforated lid, besides the cover, was used to prevent the fish from being carried out with the current, when changing the water; and the cans could be placed under a tap, or stream, if necessary, during the journey, without the fish being able to get away. The cover was also perforated, to give a free supply of air. In the transit of fish, as already stated, the most important point is to keep up a constant supply of air in the water.   It is found that water is composed of rounded globules, which admit of a certain quantity of air in the interstices.   Fish require oxygen, which they respire by their gills, which fulfil the functions of the lungs in the mammalia.   When all the air, the quantity of which is very limited, which is contained in a vessel of water, has been deprived of its oxygen by being breathed over in passing through the gills, the fish must become suffocated, as certainly as would a human being, if shut up in a close box without fresh air.   There are fish, such as the golden carp, that do not suffer in this way, as they can come to the surface and obtain a supply of oxygen, but active fish such as salmon and trout, which are accustomed to highly aerated water, in the rapid rivers, or the seas which they frequent, perish very quickly if confined in a small vessel of water without a current.   The remedy is, to give a supply of air at intervals, and the simplest and most effective method, of attaining this object, is by using a strong pair of bellows, and an indiarubber tube about two feet in length, to force the air to the bottom of the fish-cau.

The tube should be corked at the end, and pierced with a number of minute holes with a fine wire made red hot, so as to bring the air into contact with as large a surface of water as possible.   When fish turn on their sides, and are perishing for want of air, a few strokes of the bellows act upon them like magic, and they immediately recover.   In practice, I used the bellows every 15 minutes, although less frequently would probably have done equally well, but it is better to err on the safe side.

In the transport of fish, the danger increases greatly with high temperatures.   In distributing the Californian salmon, I kept them at the temperature at which they had been hatched, and to which they had afterwards been accustomed, which was 55 to 57 and occasionally up to 60 deg., and I am satisfied that my doing so, contributed greatly to the successful result which was attained.

Plenty of room in the cans is also very important, as fish will go safely in small numbers, when they would perish if crowded. It is easy to keep the temperature down to any point that may be desired, by the use of wet covers to the fish-cans, and by having a supply of ice packed in sawdust, to use on the journey. A bucket in which to wash the ice is necessary, also a thermometer, and a small net to pour the water into when liberating the fish, so as to be able to count them, and to ascertain if any have died. The net is also of great service, when the water is changed on the journey. This I should not recommend to be done on a journey of eighteen or twenty hours' duration, if the fish have plenty of room, and no food be given to them; but in a long journey the water gets foul and should then be changed. Good water from a spring or running creek free from mineral taint is the best, or rain water if good, but changing the water is somewhat dangerous; and the temperature should be carefully attended to, so as to prevent a too sudden shock to the fish. A lower temperature than 50 deg. for salmon or trout is unnecessary in transit, and if too low it may even be dangerous, and higher than 60 deg. should be avoided. Before placing the fish in the fresh water, its temperature should be brought as near as possible to that from which they have been taken, or the water brought to the desired temperature by pouring in fresh water slowly. Fish do not seem to suffer by being poured out with the water from one vessel to another, and by the use of a small net made by stretching some mosquito netting over a hoop of wire, the fish can be transferred from one can to another, and their number ascertained, by only allowing a few to go on the net with a little water at a time, and then allowing these to spring off the net, into the vessel placed ready to receive them.

Tobacco smoke is most injurious and poisonous to salmon fry in transit; especially if the bellows be used while the air is impregnated with it. The essential oil of tobacco is a volatile essence known as nicotine. It is a deadly poison, and when air filled with tobacco-smoke is forced into the cans, the nicotine is condensed and remains in the water, causing certain death to the fish should the quantity of the poison be sufficient. Even the fumes and smoke from the locomotive, may in some cases prove dangerous. I have had losses occur where the cause could not be traced; and it is singular that only a part will sometimes die, and the remainder seem unaffected. Motion of the vessel, however violent, does not seem to hurt the fish, at any rate after the first few miles of the journey, and, in fact, rather tends to benefit them, by the æration of the water, caused by its splashing about in the cans.

In sending off the different lots of fish to their destinations I gave written instructions to the attendant in the following form :—

1. Keep the water thoroughly ærated by an ærator every fifteen minutes.

2. Keep them in water of the same temperature that they have been accustomed to. This can be effected by means of ice.

3. Use the water in which they have been bred, and keep everything clean about them.

4. Take out all dead fish at least once a day, as they putrefy quickly and foul the water.

5. Give them a fresh supply of the same water if possible, or of water equally pure, every twenty-four hours, and give but little food in transit.

6. Tobacco-smoke will surely kill them.

7. Turn out about twenty or thirty in one place in shallows, and do not subject them to a too sudden change of temperature.

Abundance of space in the cans is of great importance, especially for large fish. Two thousand *alevins* have been carried successfully in a ten-gallon can, but one hundred and fifty mullet, about six inches long could not be kept alive in the same vessel, although about 30 would travel safely. Fish differ greatly in this respect; some dying at once when caught in a net. Perch and carp can be carried in wet grass or in moss for hours without injury, and in Germany are taken to market in this way, and if not sold, brought back to the ponds alive and well. Crayfish or lobsters will live out of water for a very long time, and may be taken hundreds of miles by giving them a drink occasionally. I have taken Murray lobsters from Echuca to Longerenong on the Wimmera, a great part of the way by coach, with little loss. Flounders can be carried in water with little risk, also whiting, bream, and mullet, but sand-eels, gar-fish, and trevale are very difficult to transport alive.

THE THIRD IMPORTATION OF ENGLISH SALMON OVA TO VICTORIA.

The experiments made to introduce the English salmon to Victoria not having been very conclusive, I was still desirous of making another experiment on a small scale to test the point, and, learning that the s.s. *Chimborazo* was bringing a shipment of English salmon ova for the New Zealand Government, I considered that it would be a good opportunity of ascertaining, by another experiment on a

small scale, whether the English salmon could be successfully hatched and reared in Victorian waters, and I telegraphed to Sir George Grey as follows :—" Can you spare
3,000 salmon ova, ex *Chimborazo*, for experiment here ?
Will pay cost." The reply came promptly to the following
effect :—" You can take 3,000 salmon ova from *Chimborazo*.
We cannot accept payment." This very generous offer
on behalf of the New Zealand Government, I at once
determined to accept, although as I had joined with them
in half the cost of a previous shipment by the *Durham*, I
expected that my present request would have been granted
on the same arrangement, of my paying a proportionate
part of the cost of the shipment. On the arrival of the
Chimborazo, I found that the boxes containing the ova
were carefully packed in the icehouse beneath the ice, and
that between two and three feet of ice still remained over
them. The total number of ova shipped was about 50,000,
and they were packed in 55 boxes. There was also a box
of the ova of the common trout. On the ice being removed
the boxes were handed up, and the lids of some of them
having been damaged, Mr. Howard, who came over from
New Zealand, to take charge of the ova on their transhipment into the *Alhambra*, examined the eggs by lifting up
the moss covering them, and it was at once evident, that
the great bulk of those in four of the boxes so examined,
had perished, as very few healthy ova could be seen. He
handed over to me three other boxes, with the remark
that he did not think they were worth taking away. I had
them placed in a larger box with ice above them, and took
them direct to the ice-works, where I opened them in the
ice-room, at a temperature of 32 deg. The boxes were
differently packed ; one with a Y on it, was packed by
Mr. A. Youl, and had, in addition to the moss, a layer of
charcoal at the bottom. The other two had been packed

by Mr. Frank Buckland. I picked out the ova that appeared healthy, and counted the whole of the ova in these two boxes, and found that only 270 ova remained showing any signs of vitality, out of a total of about 1,500. On the other box being opened I was delighted to find the ova bright, transparent, and of a fine pink colour. I could only find four dead ova, and did not further disturb the box. These ova were much larger, approaching in this respect to the Californian ova, and had evidently been taken at the right time from a " ripe " fish in the best condition. The other two boxes contained smaller-sized ova, of a paler colour and more irregular in form, being in many instances oval-shaped, and wanting in the bright look of healthy ova. Their appearance reminded me forcibly of my unfortunate shipment by the *Durham*, from which only five fish were hatched.

It may be remarked, that I should not " look a gift horse in the mouth," but it is only at the end of a long voyage, that defects in the mode of sending fish ova can be seen and pointed out; and if is for the benefit of all who are interested in pisciculture, that the actual facts should be made known, so that errors may be discovered and avoided in future. Whether the American pisciculturists are more experienced, or the American salmon ova are less delicate, there is no doubt that the Americans have been more successful in their shipments of ova, and that our English friends may learn something from them as to the *modus operandi*, which has given such satisfactory results. From the Californian ova being usually on the point of hatching on their reaching here, it is evident that the hatching process is advanced to a certain stage before they are shipped, which enables them to stand the voyage better, and gives the opportunity of rejecting before shipment any eggs which may perish or remain unimpregnated. It is my opinion that until this plan be adopted, no future shipments of English salmon ova can be sent, with any hope of results being obtained that will be anything like satisfactory. The voyage is now so much shortened by the great speed of the new line of fast steamers, that there is no danger of the ova hatching out on the voyage, even if the incubation be advanced to the stage when the half of the time required has elapsed.

The damage done to the broken boxes did not injure the ova ; one of these boxes had a Y on it, and the ova in it were no better than those in the others, showing that the difference was more in the ova than in the packing.

On account of the high temperature of the waters at the time, I thought it better to leave the boxes of ova in the ice-house for two or three weeks—where the process of incubation would proceed slowly—until the heat of summer was over, when they were taken to Ercildoune and placed in the hatching boxes there.

On examination of the ova it was found that only about 200 looked as if likely to hatch, these being all out of one box which had been packed by Mr. Youl. After about a fortnight these commenced to hatch, and about 150 fine healthy young fish were the result. These seemed to thrive well for a time, but after a few days became unhealthy, and commenced to die off without apparent cause. On a close examination I found that some iron pipes had been laid to carry the water through a dam, and these had been coated over with tar, as is usually done to prevent corrosion. I had this water at once cut off, and used only the spring water, which I had before refrained from using on account of its high temperature. The fish continued to die, but a few seemed to improve. They all continued to grow rapidly. Even those that showed evident tokens of being fatally attacked grew larger every day. The first symptom of the ailment was a small white spot on the umbilical sac; after this appeared the fish became dull and sluggish, and ran round in a circle. The white speck increased in size, and in about a week generally proved fatal. A few survived, and of these, thirty healthy specimens of the *salmo salar* are still alive. They have made rapid growth, and are now nearly two inches in length, and very thriving and healthy. I shall try to keep these fish in the ponds at Ercildoune until they are of the age to spawn, in the hope that some fertile ova may be obtained from them. This small number could not at any rate be expected to do much in stocking a river, taking into account all the dangers to which they would be exposed, and the experiment of retaining them in fresh water, may give some very interesting and valuable results.

EXPERIMENT OF M. COSTE IN KEEPING SALMON IN FRESH WATER.

In a note to the *Societé Imperiale d'Acclimatation* of France, dated March 4, 1859, by M. Jules Cloquet, the statement is made that salmon have been found to propagate their species in artificial ponds of fresh water. The details are of so much interest that I have made the following translation for the benefit of English readers :—
" I have the honour to make known to the Society a discovery which, it appears to me, is destined to exercise a marked influence upon the future progress of pisciculture in our rivers. I refer to the reproduction of salmon in artificial ponds securely enclosed, in which the fish, shut up from the time of hatching, have never been able to migrate to the sea. This discovery has been made at Saint Lucufa, near Saint Cloud, in one of the domains of

the Emperor, where for several years M. Coste has carried out, under the eyes of His Majesty, some extensive experiments. The little pond which has been the theatre of this curious phenomenon is situated in the hollow of a shady valley, and is only about two and a half acres in extent. Its depth is about 20 feet at the embankment, while the depth decreases gradually towards the other end, the bottom being well covered with vegetation. The water is pure and always cold, being supplied by springs from the slopes around, and is sufficiently abundant to form a cascade at the point where it overflows the reservoir. Three years ago this pond was empty while some repairs were in progress, and when the bank was closed the water soon accumulated so as to fill the reservoir. M. Coste placed in it some trout of a year old, which he had placed temporarily, under the surveillance of the Emperor, in a little pond of about six feet square. These trout are now four years old and are 19 to 22 inches in length. In April and May, 1857, several thousands of young salmon, placed for hatching at the *College de France*, two months before, were liberated in the pond with the trout, and these young salmon, notwithstanding the enemies they had there already, have succeeded so well, that when the pond was netted last month by order of the Emperor, and in the presence of their Majesties, there was caught in a single draught of the net, more than two hundred and twenty pounds weight. These fish are now twenty-two months old, weigh on the average about a quarter of a pound, and are ten to twelve inches in length. M. Coste found to his great surprise that all these fish were ready to spawn. The females had their ova matured, and some of their eggs were taken and artificially impregnated at the time. I have seen these eggs, and the embryo is so far developed that they will hatch out in a short time. The possibility of the reproduction of the salmon, in ponds where they are closely shut in, is then a fact acquired by science. It is shown here in a manner so general that it cannot be looked upon as an exception, and if nothing comes to interfere with this great experiment, the result must be yet more striking next season, when the fish have attained to a larger size.

" From this experiment, it appears also that the first spawning of the salmon takes place at eighteen months old, the same as that of the trout, and that the number of eggs of the first spawning is about two hundred. If these ova are less highly coloured than those of large fish caught in the open waters, this is probably from the flesh of the young salmon not having yet acquired the tint that it would have at a greater age. This takes away the last objection that has been made to the raising of salmon in close ponds, but to succeed in this industry, it is necessary to know how to choose conditions favorable for carrying it out."

In the experiment here described, it would have been much more satisfactory if the trout had not been present in the pond, and, singularly enough, no mention is made of their having been caught in the net with the salmon. I have tried to ascertain the final result of this interesting experiment, but have failed to find in the transactions of the Society, any further reference to it. All the authorities agree, however, that salmon detained in fresh water beyond the time of their migration to the sea, have their development checked and grow but slowly, and the possibility of obtaining matured ova from them before they go to the sea, is a curious scientific fact, rather than a discovery of much practical value. It might, however, be of some utility, where a small number of sea-going fish, were retained for the purpose of securing a further supply of ova, for their reproduction before being themselves liberated.

THE IDENTIFICATION OF SALMON AND TROUT.

When the soldiers of Cæsar in their victorious march upon Gaul and Britain, reached the banks of the Garonne, the saltatory motions of a fish new to them, making his ascent from the sea, obtained for him the specific name, that his habits so well justify to the present day, as may be well seen in any river where salmon abound ; this fish being able to leap ten or twelve feet high in ascending waterfalls on the way to its spawning ground. The *Salmo salar* is admittedly the king of fishes but there are princes and nobles of the family, which bear such a close resemblance to him, that the identification of individuals is in some cases a matter of great difficulty.

The genus *Salmo* presents such diversity of form, caused by differences in food, climate, circumstances, and the quality of the water of the streams and rivers in which the specimens are found, that the icthyologist sometimes finds the determination of the identity of individual specimens of the genus, a most difficult problem to solve. The difficulties are greater also, from the development of the sexual characters materially changing the appearance of the fish at certain seasons, the colour differing most markedly at the breeding season, and in the males, the cartilaginous protuberance which is then formed on the under jaw, completely alters their appearance. Added to this is the ascertained fact, that many, if not all, of the species are capable of hybridisation, and the hybrids have in some cases been found to be capable of propagating their kind, and of again crossing with the pure race. Hence it is not improbable, that there are intermediate forms connecting— in many cases—the different genera, and rendering identification difficult, if not impossible. The crosses between the salmon and the trout are of rare occurrence in their natural state, but by artificial impregnation this has often been effected. I have failed, however, to find any record of hybrids from this cross, having been proved to be fertile.

There are certain characters, which are found to be constant in numbers of individuals, and which are relied upon for identification of the species. These are:—the form of the bones of the checks and jaws; the size, arrangement, and permanence, or otherwise, of the teeth; the form and development of the fins; size of the scales indicated by the number of rows above and below the lateral line; the number of the vertebræ, and of the pyloric cæca, which are sac-like appendages to the main gut, which is short and simple.

There are other characters, which are found to be variable, and little reliable as a means of identifying the species, such as the number of the fin rays; the colour, form, size, number, and position of spots and bars, or parr-marks. Although the parr-marks, or transverse bars, are common to all the individual species of the genus, it has been observed that the migratory species have two or three more, than the non-migratory kinds. The males attain brighter colours than the females, as the spawning season approaches, while the young of the different migratory species put on a coat of silvery scales, which covers the bluish transverse bars, before they commence their migration to the sea.

The colour of the bottom of the water in which the fish live, as well as that of the water itself, influences greatly their appearance and markings, and, like the chameleon, they have the power, to some extent, of changing their colour in accordance with their surroundings.

The size of the fish is also a very variable character, and cannot be relied upon as a guide to its identification. It is well known that the size of trout depends on the amount and quality of their food, and the extent of the feeding-ground available.

It is stated by Gunther that the *Salmo fario*, when it inhabits a small mountain pool, with scanty food, never reaches a greater weight than eight ounces ; while, in a large lake or river, where food is abundant, it attains to a weight of fourteen or sixteen pounds. It has been found by dissection that these overgrown fish are usually barren, and hence such large specimens, from their well-known ferocity towards the young of their own species, are very objectionable amongst breeding fish.

The salmonoids that have been introduced to Australian waters, including those of Tasmania are the *Salmo salar*, *Salmo trutta*, *Salmo fario*, *Salmo eriox*, and the *Salmo quinnat*.

The *Salmo salar* has larger scales than any of the other salmonoids, and the number of rows above and below the lateral line is a means of identifying this fish. Its form is the most elegant and symmetrical of any of the genus ; and its speed and power in the water, whether for swimming or leaping up waterfalls, on its toilsome ascent to the spawning beds, is most remarkable. It attains to a length of four or five feet. It has a single longitudinal row of teeth on the vomer, or bony plate in the roof of the mouth, which are gradually lost, except three or four, commencing from behind and coming towards the front of the mouth, at an early age. The dorsal fin has fourteen rays, the anal eleven, the pectoral fourteen ; the vertebræ number fifty-nine to sixty ; the pyloric appendages are fifty-three to seventy-seven. The parr has eleven transverse bars. There are eleven or twelve rows of scales transversely from behind the adipose fin, or rayless back fin near the tail, forward to the lateral line. The young of the first and second year is called a "parr ;" after they assume the silvery coat, in twelve to twenty-four months ; they are called " smolts," in which stage the scales are very easily removed, and come off on their being handled. On their return from the sea they are called " grilse." After spawning the female is called a " kelt," and the male a " kipper."

The form of the bones of the opercular or valve-like plates covering the gills and forming the cheek-bones, affords a useful guide to identify the species, the posterior margin of those of the salmon forming nearly a semicircle, which differs in form in the other species.

The salmon trout, or *Salmo trutta*, is a small variety of salmon, the flavour of which is considered by many to equal that of the true salmon. This fish, in different stages, is often taken for the *Salmo eriox*, with which it has been confounded by some otherwise good authorities. The parr has nine or ten cross-bars, and it is known as the " orange-fin " of some rivers. In its grilse state it is called " whitling," " hirling," or " lammasman." Its flesh is of a rich pink colour in the best specimens, and it attains a length of two to three feet. It is supposed to be capable of living altogether in fresh water, although a migratory fish, and a number of them have been detained in a pond at New Norfolk, in Tasmania, for about twelve years. All the original stock have died out, but a number of breeding fish of two generations, and descended from them, are still retained, but evidently degenerate, and wanting in vigour ; and although they pair and deposit their spawn regularly every year, their progeny are delicate and difficult to rear, through having been so long deprived of access to the sea.

The fin rays are:—dorsal thirteen, anal eleven, pectoral fifteen, vertebræ fifty-nine to sixty, pyloric appendages forty-nine to sixty-one, *rarely less*. In the grilse state, the top of the dorsal and pectoral, and the hind margin of the caudal fins are black. The hind margin of the gill-cover is obtusely rounded. It has a single row of teeth on the vomer, sometimes pointing alternately to the right and left, which soon disappear, except three or four on the front of the vomer. It has fourteen to fifteen scales in an oblique line forward from behind the adipose fin to the lateral line. There are twenty-four to thirty rows of scales above, and about twenty-two below the lateral line.

Of the *Salmo fario*, or river trout, there are two varieties in Britain (besides the various lake trouts, such as the Loch Leven trout—*S. Levenensis*—which is celebrated for its fine flavour; *S. ferox*, or large lake trout, and several other species). Of these two varieties of the *Salmo fario*, one, the *Salmo fario ausonii* of Gunther, sometimes attains to a length of over thirty inches, and weighs over twenty pounds. It is found in the southern parts of England, in Sweden, and on the continent of Europe. It has thirteen to fourteen rays in its dorsal fin, ten to eleven in the anal, and thirteen in the pectoral; it has fifty-seven to fifty-eight vertebræ, and thirty-eight to forty-seven pyloric cæca. Its dentition is the most perfect of any of the genus. The body of the vomer has a double row of strong teeth either opposite or alternate, which remain through life, as in all the varieties of *Salmo fario*. There are twenty-six to thirty rows of scales above, and twenty-one below the lateral line and fifteen in an oblique, direction from behind the adipose fin forward to the lateral line.

The other variety is much smaller, and inhabits the Scotch and Irish rivers, and some of those in the northern counties of England, both forms being found in Shropshire. The smaller variety is called by Gunther the *Salmo fario gaimardi*. It has fifty-nine to sixty vertebræ, and seldom

exceeds fifteen inches in length.   It is the small burn
trout of the Highland streams, rarely weighing more than
a pound to a pound and a quarter.   It has not yet been
introduced intothe Southern Hemisphere, but the Council
of the Acclimatisation Society has taken steps to obtain,
through Mr. Frank Buckland, a shipment of the ova.   It
is likely that this fish, from its smaller size, would suit
our streams better than the larger variety, but as in
Britain it is a more northerly form, it is doubtful whether
it may stand the climate so well in Australia, owing to the
high temperature to which it would be subjected.

The "brown trout," or *S. fario ausonii*, is of exceedingly
rapid growth, equalling in this respect, if not excelling in
its early stage, that of the salmon, and it has the faculty of
adapting itself to very different conditions.   It does well
in our creeks and rivers ; it thrives in a still pond, where
there is little or no current for many months in the
summer, and it is able to live in the brackish water of the
estuaries of the Tasmanian and New Zealand rivers, when
it becomes so changed as to puzzle the *savants* as to its
identity.   It then becomes, to some extent, migratory, as
it is obliged to ascend into fresh water to spawn.   This
adaptability to circumstances, and its great size, rapid
growth, and prolific nature, besides its power of enduring
high temperatures, render it exceedingly valuable wherever
it has been introduced.

The *Salmo fario* has the most perfect dentition of any of
the salmonidæ, and the double row of teeth on the vomer
which do not become lost, as in the migratory salmonoids,
serve as one of its main distinguishing features ; and it
never assumes the silvery garb of the migratory kinds,
although at the approach of the breeding season its colours
become more brilliant and lustrous.

The *Salmo eriox (L. Sys. Nat.)*, or *S. cambricus* of
Gunther, is a migratory fish, usually known as the "bull

trout." It is similar in habits to the salmon, but its flesh is paler in colour and inferior in quality. It is known as a "pink" or "orange fin" in its parr state. It is the "sewin" of Wales, the "grey trout" of some rivers, and the salmon-peal of others. Whereas the *Salmo salar* has twenty-two to twenty-six rows of scales above the lateral line, the *Salmo trutta* twenty-four to twenty-six, the *Salmo eriox* has twenty-seven, and the *Salmo fario* twenty-six to thirty (Gunther). It is not quite equal in size and in rapidity of growth to the salmon, and is less symmetrical, and apparently not so well formed for speed, or with such fine lines, as that fish. It attains to a length of three feet. The *Salmo eriox* has fourteen rays in the dorsal fin, eleven to twelve in the anal, sixteen in the pectoral; the ventral fin has nine and the caudal nineteen rays, the numbers being constantly the same in these two fins, in all the British species enumerated; the vertebræ are fifty-nine in number, and the pyloric appendages are thirty-nine to forty-seven, *rarely more.* The scales in the smolt stage are very deciduous. There are fourteen rows in an oblique direction, from behind the adipose fin forward to the lateral line, and twenty to twenty-two below that line. The authorities differ curiously about the identification of this fish. Gunther has not been able to obtain specimens of it from Scotland, and seems to consider it indigenous to Wales and the South of England. He thinks it " quite possible " that the typical specimen figured in " Yarrell's British Fishes," " belongs to *Salmo trutta*; " and the Salmon Commissioners of Tasmania are of the opinion that the *Salmo eriox* has not been introduced into that island.

The *Salmo quinnat* has a very distinctive mark from all the other imported salmonoids. In this fish the anal fin has from fifteen to seventeen rays, while in each of the

H

three other imported species it has only eleven to twelve.
The dorsal fin has thirteen rays. The vertebræ are sixty-
six in number, and the pyloric cæca one hundred and
fifty-five.

Amid the confused and doubtful distinctions, which it
has been attempted to found, between the different species
of the salmonidæ, it is hard to find the way, which is
rendered yet more difficult, by the many hybrids between
the species which are believed to again cross with the pure
forms, thus connecting one species with another by almost
insensible gradations. The power of adaptation to circumstances being strong in the genus, many apparently new
species, have probably been formed by accidental hybrida-
tion in the first instance, and the new form has been fixed
by breeding to the same type over a long period, the new
race, from being exposed to somewhat altered conditions,
becoming apparently a distinct species.

In a preface to the sixth volume of the Catalogue to the
fishes in the British Museum, Dr. Gunther remarks:—"The
salmonidæ and the vast literature on this family offer so
many and so great difficulties to the icthyologist, that as
much patience and time are required for the investigation
of a single species, as in other fishes for that of a whole
family. The ordinary method followed by naturalists in
distinguishing and determining species is here utterly
inadequate; and I do not hesitate to assert that no one,
however experienced in the study of other families of
fishes, will be able to find his way through this labyrinth
of variations without long preliminary study, and without
a good collection for constant comparison. Sometimes
forms are met with so peculiarly and so constantly
characterised, that no icthyologist who has seen them will
deny their specific rank; but in numerous other cases, one
is much tempted to ask whether we have not to deal with

a family which, being one of the most recent creation—
no fossil true *Salmo* being known—is composed of forms
not yet specifically differentiated."

THE GROWTH AND DEVELOPMENT OF THE SALMONIDÆ.

The salmon, the trout, and sea-trout, in their early
stages, grow at nearly the same rate for the first year, the
trout being rather more advanced. In each of the three
varieties mentioned, however, the rate of growth is most
unequal in individuals of the same age. If one hundred
ova of brown trout be taken from the same fish, and
hatched out at the same time, at twelve months old, some
of the young trout will have grown to eight inches in
length, while others will not have reached four inches.
The same curious difference in the growth of individuals
has been observed in salmon and salmon trout.

In no other animal is the difference in the rate of
growth of specimens of the same age, and subject to the
same conditions, so marked as in the salmonidæ.

When the *alevins* of trout or salmon leave the shell, the
fish is about three-quarters of an inch in length. In about
three to four weeks, the yolk sac is absorbed, this result
being hastened by a higher temperature, or retarded by a
lower one. The young salmon then becomes a parr, and soon
the parr-marks can be distinguished: and at three months old,
when about two inches in length, these marks are clearly
developed. At six months old, the parrs have attained to
an average length of three inches, some having reached
four inches; at nine months old, their length is four to
five inches; and at twelve months, some will have reached
seven to seven and a half inches; while the bulk of them

н 2

remain about five to five and a half inches long, and some, even then, are not over three inches. At this stage a transformation takes place in the migratory species. The salmon parr puts on a coat of silvery scales, covering the parr-marks, which can still be seen on removing the scales, which are loosely attached, and come off easily on handling the fish.

This change takes place immediately before the fish begins its journey to the sea, and the fish is then called a smolt. It will then endeavour to leap over any obstacle that may be in the way, in its efforts to get off to the sea, and will even leap out on dry land and perish, in its instinctive desire to reach the ocean.

The smolts begin their journey at about twelve months old, or a little over that time ; but here a singular fact has been discovered. Only one-half of the salmon parrs assume the smolt dress, and migrate to the sea in the first season, the remaining half staying another year in the fresh water, and going down to the sea at about the same time of the succeeding year. It has been found that the early migrating fish are of pretty equal numbers of both sexes. The female parrs have never been found in fresh water with fully developed roe, but the male parr is sexually matured, and it is no unusual thing to see a male parr of six inches in length waiting to impregnate the ova, which are being deposited by a salmon of fifteen or twenty pounds weight.

In England, the salmon smolts commence their descent early in May, about which time the young salmon of the succeeding year are bursting their shells. The parrs which remain in the river for a second year grow very little during that time, and do not assume the smolt dress until near the time for migrating to the sea, in the following spring. It is believed that the smolts which commence their journey to the sea in May, return to the rivers to spawn in four or five months after reaching the sea, having attained a weight of four or five pounds; while their brothers and sisters of the same age remain in the river, as parrs of two or three ounces in weight. The young salmon, on its first return from the sea, is called a "grilse;" after it has deposited its spawn, it falls off in condition, and is then unfit for the table, and loses greatly in weight. It returns to the sea, and on its next ascent, in the following season, is called a "salmon," and will then weigh ten or twelve pounds. It is believed that the transformations and habits of the *Salmo trutta* and *Salmo eriox* are similar to those of the true salmon, but these fish do not attain to the same size.

The *Salmo salar*, when detained in fresh water, has its growth greatly checked. In Scotland, some salmon fry, three to four inches long, were put in a pond, in April, 1831, some of which were caught in the summer of 1833, two to three pounds weight. The flesh was of the best colour, but rather pale.

From experiments made by Mr. Shaw, who was head keeper to the Duke of Buccleuch, at Drumlanrig Castle, the rate of growth of the salmon has been clearly ascertained, by marking the smolts with silver wire, or by notches on the adipose fin, to identify them on their return from the sea, and many disputed questions about the salmon have thus been set at rest.

It was for a long period believed that the parr was a distinct fish from the salmon, although the absence of ova in any individual instance was a strong argument against this supposition.

Salmon increase in size every succeeding year, and it was no uncommon thing at one time to get salmon of thirty pounds weight, but few of that size are now caught, as they are killed long before they attain to this weight. They have been caught 40 lbs., 50 lbs., 60 lbs. ; and one of the enormous weight of 83 lbs. is recorded.

The *Salmo fario ausonii,* or large brown trout, grows to about six inches in length in twelve months, and specimens of seven or eight inches long may be produced in that time by high feeding. In two years they will measure about fourteen inches, and weigh a pound; in three years, about three to four pounds; in four years, about four to five pounds; and in five years they will weigh six or seven pounds ; and I have caught two of that age at Ercildoune, which weighed eleven pounds each. Their growth is influenced greatly by the space they have to roam over, and the quantity of food which is available. Heat stimulates their growth, and warm water will produce larger fish than cold. A large pond will also produce larger fish than a small one. Fish artificially fed, and well cared for, will grow much faster than those that have to seek their food in the natural way. The largest trout that there is any record of having been caught in Victoria is one of about fifteen and a half pounds, which came out of Lake Learmonth, but in Tasmania brown trout of over twenty pounds have been taken.

Salmon and trout that are well fed will usually spawn at about the age of twenty-two months ; but some trout will spawn when they are only about a year old.

The hybridisation of the different species of salmonoids has been tried successfully, and the hybrids are found to be fertile in every case where they have been observed.

In a paper read before the *Societé d'Acclimatation* of France, in September, 1877, by M. Rico, director of the establishment of pisciculture of Ruisseau (*Seine-et-Oise*), details are given of a remarkable experiment, in which the eggs of the *ombre-chevalier*—a salmonoid inhabiting several of the Swiss lakes, with habits similar to that of the *Salmo fario*—were fecundated with the milt of the salmon trout. These ova were hatched in January, 1873, and the *alevins* had grown rapidly, being, at the age of six months, three and a half inches long; at twenty-two months, averaging seven inches; at thirty-four months, eleven and a half inches; and at forty-two months, over thirteen inches. The females of this new variety produced eggs at the age of twenty-two months; but as the males had already shed their milt, that of a male trout was used to fertilise the eggs, and these were hatched successfully; and the *alevins* made more rapid growth than trout of the same age, and continued to thrive in a way that indicated a robust constitution. This is an instance of the ease with which even dissimilar kinds of salmonoids can be hybridised, and the progeny not being unfertile indicates a near relationship between the two species. In these experiments, what is called the "dry" system of fertilisation of the ova was practised—that is, the ova and the seminal fluid were brought in contact in a pan, without being immersed in water. This system, which was first discovered in Russia, has produced a larger percentage of fertile eggs than the old method of fertilisation in water.

On the 1st August of this year (1878) I examined the different small salmonoids in my ponds at Ercildoune. The Californian salmon had been some time ago divided into two lots, and placed in two small ponds, the larger sized fish in one and the smaller in another. Both lots were regularly fed with liver in the same way. I measured the largest and smallest in each lot, and found in one that the largest fish was 4¼ inches in length, and the smallest 3½ inches. In the other lot the largest was 4¼ inches long and the smallest 3 inches. These fish are now about eight months old, but those that I retained were the largest and

best fish, or there would have been a much greater difference in their sizes.

These fish are silvery white on the belly and sides, and
have eleven or twelve bluish parr-marks very clearly
distinguishable. The back has three rows of very dark
green round spots about eighteen in number, and numerous
small greenish-brown spots above the lateral line. The
pectoral, ventral, and anal fins are white in colour, the
caudal, dorsal, and adipose fins are dusky on their outer
margins.

The young *Salmo salar* from the ova presented by
Sir George Grey and brought in the *Chimborazo* are
1½ inches in length, and show the parr-marks distinctly.
Their growth is very slow at present from the low
temperature of the water, the spring at which they are
placed having been swamped by surface water and the
temperature reduced to 47 deg.

I carefully examined the salmonoids bred from Tasmanian ova. They were caught in a net and drafted into
two well marked varieties, and probably one of these
could be again divided into two kinds, although, until
further developed, it is difficult to do so at present.

The largest variety is a gray coloured trout, with no red
spots excepting one faint row along the lateral line. These
fish have made much more rapid growth than the others
of the same age. The largest specimen measured 8¼ inches,
and the smallest 5¼ inches. The parr marks are slightly
distinguishable only in the smaller specimens. The pectoral, ventral and anal fins are yellow, the dorsal has three
rows of black spots, the caudal has a black margin, and
the adipose fin is of a pink colour on the tip. A specimen
sent to Professor M'Coy was pronounced by him to belong
to *Salmo trutta*. The fin rays are—

D., 12 ; A., 10 ; P., 13 ; pyl. cæc. 63.

There are fourteen rows of scales from behind the adipose fin forward to the lateral line, and twenty-five rows above the lateral line. None of these fish have yet commenced to put on their silvery coat.

The smaller Tasmanian salmonoids measure from $3\frac{1}{2}$ inches to $5\frac{1}{2}$ inches. The dorsal fin has two or three rows of bright red spots, intermixed with a few black ones. The adipose fin is of a deep red colour. The caudal fin has red tips slightly tinged with black at the extremities. The pectoral, ventral, and anal fins are yellow. There are eleven to thirteen parr-marks plainly distinguishable. On the sides and back are many bright red spots, intermixed with black ones. Two of this size, which had assumed the silvery coat at about ten months old were unfortunately carried away by a flood. They were of more elegant form than the others, and distinct in appearance. Their length was about 5 inches. The scales did not appear to be deciduous. The parr-marks were almost covered by the silvery scales. The dorsal and caudal fins had a dusky margin. These two fish had been placed in a small pond by themselves that their development might be easily observed. Some of these fish are probably *Salmo fario*, and a few may prove to be *Salmo salar*, as the two silvery fish which escaped probably were. The warmth of the water, together with high feeding, have caused a rapid development and growth of these fish, especially the *Salmo trutta*, which are much farther advanced than fish of the same age in England; although the milt in the males which were examined was not yet developed. The Tasmanian fish above referred to were about eleven months old when examined on the 1st of August.

AQUICULTURE.

Water is one of the natural elements which, next to the air we breathe, is of the most importance to the human race. It makes an easy highway for civilisation to extend her bounds to the remotest corners of the earth. As a source of power it is invaluable; as a fertilising agent it is of the utmost benefit to all kinds of animal and vegetable life; but it is in the point of view as an element for the habitation and cultivation of useful fishes, that we would at the present time wish to deal with it. In this aspect it becomes mainly important, as furnishing a healthy, nourishing, and very welcome and delicious addition to our food supply.

It is asserted as an undoubted fact, that an acre of water well stocked with fish, will produce a far larger amount of food for man, than the same extent of the best land, and with a far less expenditure of labour; and it is only in old countries, such as China, where the population has over-taken the food supply of the land, that the waters are cultivated as they ought to be, and that fish becomes a main element in the daily food of the mass of the people. With the possibility of obtaining by scientific aids and appliances, such valuable results from the waters of our streams, rivers, and lakes, and even from the seas which wash our shores, the subject of aquiculture is deserving of our earnest attention. The enormous fecundity of all kinds of fish, renders their increase and multiplication easy; and the knowledge of how to turn to the best account this bounty of nature, is a study worthy of the highest intel-lectual powers, and will well repay those who devote their time and attention to it, by results of a kind valuable to the nation.

M. Eugene Simon, who acted as French Consul in China, gives some interesting information, as to the extent to which aquiculture is carried on in China, and we should not be above taking a lesson even from the "heathen Chinee," whom it is the fashion in these days to despise.

M. Simon, in describing the manner in which the waters of China are utilised, states that their fertility is so great that " the streams and rivers, the lakes and canals, with which two-thirds of China is covered, literally swarm with fish, butchers' meat being no more indispensable. It is impossible to form an idea of this fecundity. It is not only in the watercourses that they fish, but in the rice-fields, and in ponds which retain water for a time after heavy rains ; and if we add, that there are varieties of fish which increase so prodigiously that they spawn twice in one month, you would not be surprised that fish is sold for one penny per pound, and the most costly at fivepence or sixpence. They fish with nets of all sizes and dimensions, with ground-lines, with tridents, and with cormorants. Fish is the habitual nourishment of about 350 millions of inhabitants, and remains always abundant."

Many of the curious and valuable fish found in China would, no doubt, be worthy of introduction here. In a recent number of *Nature*, reference is made to "M. Darby de Thiersant, a French *charge d' affaires*, who has been instrumental in introducing a number of Chinese plants and animals into his native country, and has made arrangements for the importation in quantities of the Sitz, one of the most valued fish found in Chinese waters. The fish belongs to the carp family, and when fed on sea plants in ponds attains with great rapidity a weight of about 40lb. During the past three years experiments which were made on the fish in the *Jardin d' Acclimatation*, have shown it to be well adapted to a European climate; and, as it increases rapidly, it is to be hoped that within a few years it can be introduced extensively throughout Europe." Let us hope that Australia also may soon obtain this valuable fish. We have at command however, many useful varieties, which, by a little care and attention, might be multiplied immensely, such as the carp, tench, perch, and trout.

Of desirable fish to introduce and acclimatise in our waters the Gouramier is one of the best, and is said to be most excellent for the table. Some specimens were brought here some years ago by Mr. Joshua, from Mauritius, which arrived in a healthy state ; but from some cause unknown, probably the coldness of the water, they all perished the first night after being landed. This fish requires a warm climate, and would probably succeed in the lagoons of the northern parts of the colony, and of Riverina.

The *Coregonus Albus*, or white fish of the North American lakes, is a fish of great value for the table. It is called the Gizzard fish of Canada. It rarely exceeds a foot and a half in length, and a weight of five pounds. From its small mouth it is not dangerous to other fish, its food being insects, larvæ, &c. It is well worthy of introduction, and would succeed best in the colder districts of the colony.

There is an Egyptian fish called the Binny, which is most highly esteemed in that country. It is found in the upper and lower Nile, where it is very abundant. It is celebrated for the excellence of its flesh, and a proverbial saying, attributed to the fish is:—"If you know a better than I, do not eat me." There are fishermen at Syout and Kené, who have no other occupation than fishing for the Binny. M. Geoffry St. Hilaire has identified this fish with the famous *Lepidotus* of the ancients, and which, according to Strabo, was the only fish which, together with the *Oxyrhyncus*, was worshipped as sacred all over Egypt. The Binny grows to about twenty inches long, but specimens of three feet in length are not uncommon. It is remarkable for the silvery lustre of its scaly coat, which distinguishes it from all the other fish of the Nile. It is one of the cyprinoids, allied to the Barbel, and would be a most valuable acquisition to our waters.

In our great salt lakes a vast field is open for a grand experiment in the introduction of the most valuable kinds of sea-fish. This idea occurred to me more than three years since, and I determined should the experiment seem likely to prove successful, to make the attempt to introduce sea-fish into Lake Corangamite, which is the largest lake in the colony, having an area of about fifty thousand acres. I proposed the matter to Mr. J. H. Connor, who formerly represented that district in the Legislative Assembly, and who had gone to much trouble in conveying various kinds of fresh-water fish to stock the streams and lagoons near Colac and I offered to pay the cost of an experiment with the desired object in view. He very heartily entered into my scheme, and, as a preparatory measure, obtained from the Government Analytical Chemist, Mr. Johnson, an analysis of the water of Lake Corangamite. Samples were taken at three different places, which, however, did not vary much from each other. The water contained some earthy impurities which were not taken into account, and the following soluble salts. One imperial gallon yields :—

Chloride of sodium (common salt)	...	1280	grains
Sulphate of sodium	... ...	43	„
Carbonate of sodium	... ...	35	„
Total	... ...	1358	grains

Mr. Johnston states that, in his opinion, " this water can be safely trusted not to injure a great variety of fish, the foreign substances present being of the most innocent nature."

This analysis being encouraging, Mr. Connor started with a lot of various kinds of sea-fish from Geelong, a proportion of which reached Corangamite alive, and seemed to enjoy being liberated in their new home. I then placed a further sum at Mr. Connor's disposal, to enable him to place a larger number and a greater variety of fish in the lake; and six different trips were made; and although many died on the way, a large number of fish of a size that indicated the prospect of their soon spawning, were placed in the lake. Mr. Connor wrote to say that he wished to bear the cost of the first trip, but as he had given his personal care to the experiment all through in the most generous way, I did not think that he should bear any part of the actual outlay. The first lot was placed in the lake on the 3rd of June, 1876, and the last lot on the 25th of June, 1878. The result of this most interesting experiment is not yet known, as, in a lake twenty miles in length, a few fish are not easily found again. There is abundance of food, however, in its waters, including a small shrimp and a kind of whitebait, (*Galaxias Attenuatus*), which is found in myriads coming up to spawn in its tributaries, and as the water of the lake has been proved by chemical analysis to differ little from sea water, and to contain nothing deleterious to fish life, it is highly probable that the attempt will be successful. The fish included in the experiment, and liberated alive, have been the following:—

Name of fish.	Number liberated.
Whiting—*Sillago Punctata*	9
Flounder—*Pleuronectes Victoriæ*	47
Mullet—*Dajaus Diemensis*	108
Bream—*Caranx Georgianus*	12
Crayfish—*Astacus*	8
Travale—*Neptonemus Travale*	
Roughy—*Arripis Georgianus*	1
Salmon Trout—*Arripis Truttaceus*	27
Flathead—*Platycephalus Richardsoni*	25
Gurnet—*Trigla Polyommata*	4
Oyster—*Ostrea*	384

Some travale and sand-eels died on the way, being very
difficult to carry. I accompanied the fish, and saw them
liberated on the last occasion.; and, with a few exceptions,
they soon recovered from the effects of the journey. The
oysters were of several varieties. About 350 live fish were
placed in the lake out of about 1000, being a loss of two-
thirds on the journey. This loss was mainly caused by
putting too many in some of the cans, and from the want
of the bellows in the earlier experiments, to ærate the
water. Some of the kinds experimented upon could not
be taken there alive. On the last occasion I watched with
particular attention one trevale, which had a can to itself,
but which, with every possible care, died before reaching
Corangamite. Oysters can, of course, be carried to any
distance in safety. Those deposited in the lake were
placed in a most favourable spot, on both sides of a ruined
stone wall, running about half a mile into the water, where
the loose stones will afford good holding ground for the
spat, should the oysters live and deposit their spawn
there. A portion of them were also put in some rocky
ground, on the west side of the lake. The numbers of
fish given are those that were placed alive in the lake out
of three lots, details of some of the other trips not being
obtainable. A few carp, perch, trout, and Californian
salmon I have also placed in some of its tributaries, which
may, at some future time, become of value, and it will be
most interesting to watch the result.

It is stated by residents in the neighborhood, that the
waters of Lake Corangamite have been gradually rising for
the last ten years. This is, no doubt, owing to the extensive works by which many swamps and marshy places have
been freed from surplus water and drained so as to become
better fitted for pasturage. This increase in the quantity
of water in the lake, should it continue, will inevitably

cause its waters to overflow into its natural outlet in the
Barwon river. Hitherto the evaporation over its large
surface has balanced the drainage flowing into it, so that
no overflow has occurred, but should its waters rise so as
to overflow every season, the amount of salt carried away
would necessarily cause the water of the lake to become
fresher every year, and it would be interesting to know
whether the sea-fish introduced there, could adapt themselves to the gradual change from salt to fresh water,
which would then take place.

Our oyster-fisheries, that were once productive, have now
failed almost entirely, and we are dependent upon other
colonies for supplies of that delicious bivalve. Why should
not scientific culture restore the productiveness of our old
oyster-beds, and, with the knowledge so easily attainable,
by the aid of tiles and fascines, establish fresh beds on
suitable parts of the bays and indentations of our coast
line ?

The more careful protection of small and immature fish
and a close time, rigorously enforced, to protect migratory
fish during the spawning season, would save valuable kinds,
such as the delicious fresh water herring or grayling
(prototroctes maræna, Gunther), now threatened with extinction, and would allow of the natural increase, which
is now prevented to a great extent by a wasteful system of
killing small fish, and of netting breeding fish on the way
to their spawning grounds.

In France great efforts have been made to cultivate the
waters, and a department was created, with an establishment at Huningue, under the care of M. Coste, which has
greatly increased the value of the fisheries of the country.

An attempt made in 1877 to introduce the Californian
salmon into France proved unsuccessful. Two hundred
thousand ova were sent from America, but on their arrival

they were found to have perished. It is to be hoped that a renewed effort will be made to acclimatise this valuable fish in the rivers of France.

The waters of the Mediterranean have no salmon in them, and probably the *Salmo salar* would not live in the high temperatures of that sea, but it is extremely probable that the Californian salmon would be well suited to the European rivers which debouche into its waters. During the last season three hundred thousand eggs of this fish were imported by the German Fischerei-Verein, and on their arrival twenty-five thousand of them were found to be in good condition. A portion of the fish hatched from these ova were put into the tributaries of the Danube, and the remainder into those of the Rhine. There are many rivers and streams falling into the Mediterranean, in France, Italy, Austria, Spain, and Portugal which might be found well suited to the Californian salmon, and the attempt to introduce this valuable fish would be well worthy of the attention of the governments of the countries interested. The Rhone and its tributaries should be especially well suited for this experiment; also the Po and Adige in Italy, the Ebro and Guadalquiver in Spain, and the Tagus and Guadiana in Portugal, besides many other minor streams of little note, but from which valuable results might be obtained.

In the United States of America the subject has been warmly taken up by an enlightened Government, and enormous numbers of fish have been hatched artificially and afterwards liberated, greatly increasing thereby the annual results of the fisheries, which had been gradually diminishing, and which tended towards the extinction of the most valuable kinds. The matter is necessarily the business of the Government, as no individual can be expected to breed fish on a large scale, and to liberate

I

them in open waters, where he cannot hope to reap the benefit resulting from his labours.

In Canada and Nova Scotia establishments for the re-stocking of the waters by the artificial incubation of fish have been in operation for some time.

In a letter just received from Sir Robert Officer, Chairman of the Tasmanian Salmon Commissioners, very encouraging accounts are given of the success of the *salmonidæ* introduced into that colony. He says :—" I have just had the pleasure of receiving your note, in which you ask for a further supply of ova, and in reply I beg to assure you that everything in our power will be done to meet your wishes. We have this season the prospect of a very large produce of ova and young fish, both in the ponds, and in the Plenty River adjoining, as well as in the other tributaries of the Derwent. The rills connected with the ponds, and the bed of the Plenty for several miles of its course, may be seen thickly studded with the *redds* of the fish, in which will be found, I doubt not, the whole three species of *salmonidæ* in vast numbers. The Plenty is but one of the many fine streams connected with the Derwent, in which it is scarcely to be questioned that the same promising state of things at this moment exists. The spectacle is one that would delight you to behold."

In Scotland, that of Stormontfield on the Tay, and one at Oughterard in Galway, have produced valuable results. Norway and Sweden have their fish-hatching establishments ; Russia and Denmark have theirs at Nikolskoi and Viborg. Germany has now obtained Huningue, and Austria has a piscicultural establishment at Salzbourg. Italy has for ages cultivated her lagoons at Comacchio. While all these nations have learned the value and profit to be realised from the cultivation of their waters and seas, shall Australia remain inactive ? The same enterprise which has in a few years raised noble cities where formerly, under the shadow of the Eucalyptus and Casuarina, only a few bark mia-mias of a native race were seen, can and will advance in the culture of the waters of this new continent, until, as knowledge extends, the rivers, streams, lakes, and seas shall teem with the scaly denizens of the deep.

THE VALUE OF SALMON FISHERIES.

It is undoubtedly in the cold regions of the north that we must look for the home of the salmon. Sir John Ross, in his Arctic explorations, found salmon so abundant that he could buy one hundred pounds weight from the Esquimaux for a knife, and enormous quantities were consumed by this people, one having been observed by him to dispose of a stone weight at a meal.

Few nations have been so highly favoured as Scotland in respect to their salmon fisheries, but unfortunately, for want of proper legislation to protect the spawning fish, the value of the fisheries has greatly diminished; and should there not be greater attention paid to this question, and sufficient protection given to the fish, there is a risk of the extinction of the salmon in some of those rivers where they formerly abounded.

In Norway, salmon is also extremely abundant, and in the rivers of the Pacific sea-board of North America, the salmon fisheries are wonderfully productive, the rivers in these countries not having been closely fished till recently. The extension of railways and of rapid steam communication by sea, by bringing the salmon rivers within reach of markets, has caused that fish to become scarce, and like the deer and other wild game, it would no doubt soon disappear altogether unless protected by wise legislation.

In a work entitled "The Salmon," by Mr. Alexander Russell, it is stated that the annual value of three Scotch fishery districts, "the Tay, the Spey, and the twin rivers entering the sea at Aberdeen, amounts to nearly £40,000, and from the reports of the Irish Commissioners we learn that in 1862 three Irish railways conveyed 900,000 lbs. of salmon, being equal in weight and treble in value to 15,000 sheep. In Scotland, the Tay alone furnishes annually about 800,000 lbs., being equal in weight and treble in value to 13,000 sheep. The weight of salmon produced by the Spey is equal to the weight of mutton annually yielded to the butcher by each of several of the smaller counties."

According to the same authority the value of the Irish fisheries has been stated semi-officially at £200,000 a year. In Britain a salmon fishery is as saleable a property as houses or land, and is often held by as ancient a title. The fisheries of the Duke of Richmond on the Spey are worth about £13,000 annually, and the right to fish in a river often lets for a larger rental, than that of a considerable extent of land on each of its banks.

In the Oregon territory of the United States, the produce of the fisheries is worth seven or eight hundred thousand pounds annually, and in 1875, sixteen millions of of pounds of tinned fish, were prepared for exportation. The exports of preserved salmon from the Columbia river and its tributaries in 1877, were so much increased as to be estimated at a value of a million sterling.

It is evident, therefore, that if the experiment of introducing the salmon into Australian waters should prove successful, very valuable pecuniary results may follow in a not very remote future, besides the sport which will be afforded, and which is not the least of the advantages to be expected from the undertaking. There are good grounds for the belief, that the introduction of the salmon is not merely a curious scientific experiment, but that there is a prospect of its proving useful, in adding materially to the food supply of the people.

THE DISTRIBUTION AND LIBERATION OF THE CALIFORNIAN SALMON FRY.

When the salmon fry had nearly advanced to the stage in which the umbilical sac is absorbed, I found it necessary to make arrangements for their distribution without delay. While yet in the *alevin* stage, no food is required, and they need less room in the cans in which they are conveyed, than when they have grown to a larger size. I had many applications for a portion of the fry, for various rivers and streams, from shire and borough councils, and from private individuals; and after collecting as much information as possible, concerning the various rivers and streams in the colony, I came to the conclusion that the Gippsland rivers, and those streams running into the sea near Cape Otway, were the best suited for the purpose. The Yarra River, also, notwithstanding that its waters are sometimes poisoned by the noxious refuse from many factories, will, I think, prove well suited to the Californian salmon, as their descent and ascent would probably take place after a flood, which would have purified the few miles of the river near Melbourne most dangerous to them. And a swift-swimming fish, that can go thirty miles up the stream in a day, will go through the most dangerous part of the river, opposite Melbourne, in a few hours. It is impossible to foresee the result of experiments of this kind in a new country, and under new conditions. We have instances of animals introduced here succeeding in the most wonderful way, and of others which seem to promise equally well, but which utterly fail, so that the test of experiment is the safest guide.

It is only about sixty years since that a salmon of twenty pounds weight was caught in the Thames, near Windsor, notwithstanding that the sewage from millions of people living on its banks was allowed to flow into it, and salmon have been re-introduced into that river by Mr. Frank Buckland within the last few years, with a good prospect of success.

The following account of the successful conveyance of the first lot of about 4000 salmon fry from Ercildoune to the Gellibrand River, a fine stream running into the sea some miles to the westward of Cape Otway, was sent by me to the *Argus* of December 20th, 1877, on my return from the trip, which was to me one of great enjoyment :—

"I have just returned from the Cape Otway ranges, where I have been distributing the first lot of the young salmon in the fine streams of that district. I placed the fish in four cans, each capable of containing about ten gallons of water, about 2000 fish in each can, at about two p.m. on Monday. The fish were lifted from the hatching-boxes with a small net, and placed in a pan containing water, which was poured into the cans from time to time, the fish being carried along with the water. A current was kept up in the cans by a stream from a hose, and syphons from one can to the other, the cans being at different levels.

" At half-past four it was time to start for the railway station. The cans were placed in the express waggon, and protected from the sun and air by thick, padded covers, and the temperature slightly lowered by placing pounded ice in the water. The water in the cans was aerated every fifteen minutes by using a pair of bellows and a piece of indiarubber tube, corked at the end, and pierced with small holes, to bring the air which was forced into the water into contact with as large a surface as possible. Fortunately, the weather, though warm, was not oppressive, and it was not difficult, by the occasional use of ice, to keep the temperature of the water from rising, and this ranged at from 54 deg. to 58 deg. throughout the journey. On my arrival at Geelong, Mr. Le Souef was waiting to take charge of two cans containing about 4000 salmon, intended for the Upper Yarra. These, on being examined at Geelong, were found to be strong and lively. On reaching the Barwon at Winchelsea, 200 were given to the station-master, who started off in the moonlight to put them in the river about 200 yards off. At Birregurra station Mr. Strachan, the occupant of Sir C. Sladen's Ripplevale estate, took charge of a small can containing 500 of the fry to place them in the upper waters of the Barwon River. On reaching Colac, at twelve p.m., the cans were transferred to an express waggon, and we at once started for the Gellibrand River by moonlight, so as to lose no time, and to get through in the cool of the night. The road was a pretty good bush track for some miles till we reached the forest, but as we penetrated further it became more difficult for a wheeled vehicle to get along, owing to fallen logs, ruts, stumps, and the steep ranges and gullies which had to be crossed. At daybreak we reached a hill just above the channel of Love's River, which is the first tributary of the Gellibrand. As the descent was very steep, and much encumbered with fallen timber, we camped, and waited for daylight, much enjoying a bush meal, by the light of an enormous fire. Our pioneers then cleared a practicable track, and after some difficulty we reached the bank of the stream, and on examination found

the salmon were lively and well. A few hundreds were
distributed up and down the river in shallows, and a few
hundreds more, in a small creek falling into Love's or
Porcupine River. Following down Love's River, a few
hundred more, were liberated in a beautiful stream called
the Trout River. The creek was swarming with a native
trout (*galaxias*), which is said to be peculiar to this
stream. It is a pretty, spotted fish, growing to about six
inches in length, and said to be of excellent flavour.
These trout are not at all shy, and will rise to the fly, and
afford good sport. I tried to get a specimen, but, having
no proper appliances, did not succeed. I was somewhat
alarmed at the prospects of the young salmon, amongst so
many strange fish, and, after liberating twenty or thirty in
a little pool, I sent the men up the stream to distribute
the rest of the lot, and sat down to watch how they would
get on in their new home.   On being turned out, the parrs
at once turned up-stream bravely, and swam about,
examining curiously what must have seemed very new to
them.   There were about a dozen native trout about three
inches long in the little pool, and the young salmon showed
their high breeding, in entering the society of these strangers
in the most self-possessed manner. The trout, on seeing
the strangers come near, darted away as if startled, but
after a little they returned, and finding the salmon coming
beside them again, one turned and darted at an intruder,
who soon showed that he was thoroughbred as far as speed
was concerned, by quickly getting away out of danger, and
I came to the conclusion that the young salmon would
soon be able to take care of themselves.

  " After a few hours of very heavy work, through a dense
scrub of mimosa, melaleuca, and ferns, underneath the tall
stems of the forest gums, we reached the bank of the
Gellibrand River about ten o'clock, and liberated the

remainder of the fish, partly in a fine creek on the south
side of the valley, and partly in the main river. The stream
was running with a clear and rapid current, about twenty
yards wide, and is greatly encumbered with fallen timber,
which bridges the channel over in many places. The
temperature of the water was 60 deg. Fahrenheit. The
river banks are lined with Eucalypti of an enormous height,
straight and round as if turned in a lathe, up to 200 feet
without a branch. Underneath are giant fern-trees,
Dicksonias, Alsophyllas, and splendid Todeas, with brush-
wood, climbers, and ferns six or eight feet high, and
very difficult to penetrate. The soil on the river flats is
good enough for anything, and the wonder is, that it is not
already occupied.

"The fish were netted out of the cans, and at the last
the water was poured through a net that any dead fish
might be seen. In one can there were nine dead, and in
the other ten, being a loss of nineteen in all out of 4000, or
less than one-half per cent. This result is exceedingly
satisfactory."

The fish taken charge of at Geelong by Mr. Le Souef
were liberated on the same day, the following particulars
having appeared in the *Argus* :—

"The deposit of salmon fry in the head waters of the
Yarra was successfully carried out yesterday morning
(December 19th, 1877). Four cans of fish were despatched
from Ercildoune on Monday, and divided at Geelong into
two lots. One lot was sent westward, and two cans were
brought on to Melbourne. They reached Spencer-street
station at eleven p.m., whence they were taken by Mr. Le
Souef, the hon. secretary of the Zoological and Acclimatisation Society (accompanied by Mr. Purchas, one of the
vice-presidents), to the Badger Creek. The party travelled
all night, and reached Coranderrk, at the junction of the

Yarra and the Badger, at seven a.m. The fish were carried
in two large cans not unlike, in shape and size, the vessels
commonly employed by milk-vendors. By the application
of ice, the temperature of the water was kept low, and air
was injected at intervals by means of a pair of bellows and
a perforated indiarubber tube. Mr. Le Souef's party
halted a short time at Coranderrk, where additional assistance was obtained, and then drove more than a mile
further up the creek. The Badger is a stream which
enters the Yarra on the north side, and is the next
tributary above the Watts River. No introduced fish have
hitherto been placed in the creek, and it is inhabited by no
more dangerous residents than the black-fish. Trout were
put into the Watts some years ago, and they have since
been caught there in considerable numbers. Cod frequent
the Yarra below the Watts, but the Badger is perfectly
free from inhabitants likely to prove unfriendly to the
young salmon. Two places about a quarter of a mile
apart, were selected for the deposit of the fry, and the
operation of ladling them from the cans into the stream
was successfully got through before ten o'clock. The fish
were in splendid condition, for not more than two dozen
(out of several thousands) were found dead. As soon as
the fry were liberated, they showed themselves to be lively
and strong, and swam about in little shoals, with their
heads up-stream, evidently pleased with their new quarters.
They averaged about two inches in length. A clear mountain creek like the Badger may be regarded as an excellent
nursery. Should the grown fish be able, when they set
out for the sea, to pass through the foul water which fills
the river in the neighbourhood of Melbourne, a problem of
great importance will be happily solved. It is believed
that, with the assistance of a seasonable freshet, which they
will probably wait for, the salmon will make their way

easily into the bay. Similarly, a freshet will help them up
again when they want to return to the head waters of the
river. So much more important must it be, to domesticate
the salmon close to the metropolis, than in the distant
rivers of Gipps Land, that the few thousand fry risked in
the present experiment, may be considered well laid out.
If success crowns the undertaking, the river will become
well stocked in the course of a few years."

The following is a very interesting letter from Mr.
Arthur King, who very generously undertook the task of
conveying 4000 salmon fry to the Latrobe River. That
he was not more successful was certainly from no want of
care or attention on his part, as his letter shows that he
did not shrink from any hardships in carrying out his
undertaking. I had intended to have accompanied Mr.
King, but my Parliamentary duties prevented my doing so.

I inspected the fish at Spencer-street, on their arrival
from Burrumbeet, and saw at once that they were not
doing well, and that many were dead, and others floating
on their sides in a sickly state. I at once concluded that
they had not had sufficient air, and on trying the bellows
and tube, found them to work but poorly, although they
were not altogether inefficient. I then used the garden
syringe vigorously for ten minutes, but did not see the
usual revival take place, which generally follows when the
fish have been suffering from want of oxygen, and I could
not make out the cause. I am satisfied that there was no
want of care in aerating the water in transit. It appeared,
however, that the train was very crowded, and some six or
seven passengers had got into the van with the salmon
cans, and that they were smoking while the bellows was
being used. I am quite certain that the nicotine poison in
the fumes of the tobacco, and nothing else, was the cause
of the loss of these 2500 salmon fry.

" Sir Samuel Wilson.

" My dear Sir,—At eleven p.m. on Thursday, 20th December, two cans, containing about 2000 each of the young salmon, were received by myself and a friend (Mr. Elliott), who volunteered to assist me in taking the salmon to the sources of the Latrobe River.

" Unfortunately, when they reached Melbourne (as you yourself saw), the fish appeared to have suffered on the journey from Ercildoune, in consequence of a defect in the bellows used to infuse fresh air into the cans. Garden syringes had, happily, been provided, by your instructions, in case of accident to the bellows apparatus, and by their means, as well as by the use of the defective bellows, the water had been aerated.

" We started from Melbourne in one of Messrs. Cobb and Co.'s express waggons, and reached Oakleigh at a quarter past one a.m. on Friday, the 21st. Syringes were used throughout the journey, in order, if possible, to revive the fainting fish.

" An express train having been provided by the Government, the fish were taken on to the Bunyip, which was reached before three a.m.

" In the train sedulous efforts were used, both with the bellows and tube, and with syringes, to aerate the water in the cans, and a considerable number of dead fish were removed.

" At three a.m. a start was made from the Bunyip in one of Messrs. Cobb and Co.'s four-horse coaches, I using one syringe, and Mr. Elliot another, occupying the whole time in aerating the water as well as we could while the coach was jolted on the road. The Latrobe River was reached at the crossing-place to Walhalla, about five miles from Shady Creek, on the Gippsland-road, at eight o'clock in the morning.

" The night had been cool throughout, and the temperature in the cans had never exceeded 53 deg. Fahr.   There was, therefore, no 'need to use the ice, which had been supplied liberally by the Melbourne Ice Company, in aid of the experiment.

"The river temperature was found not to exceed 55 deg. in the warmest place.

" The anxious time had arrived to ascertain how many fish were left alive, after so many had been removed when dead.   The journey had been hastened, so as to give a chance to some of the fish to reach their destination alive.

" Counting them carefully, we placed 1500 live fish in various parts of the river.

" Each lot was about 100 in number, and as the little swimmers found themselves at large in their new home, they moved about, as if wonderingly, but not in fear, and then gradually took their course in the shallows near the bank, in every case making their way up the stream.

"The river was clear, and running with a strong current, over a sandy bed, through a valley overhung with immense gum trees, blackwood trees, and other growth.   Fern trees were growing near the stream.

" Mr. Needham, one of the few residents in the neighbourhood, met the coach on its arrival, and kindly assisted in carrying the cans, and placing the fish in the river.   He stated that the only fish caught in that part of the river were fine black-fish and a few eels.   The swift-swimming salmon have, therefore, nothing to fear from such sluggish neighbours.

" In passing various watercourses, I found the residents in the neighbourhood anxious to have some of the fish left at each ; but as there was a doubt whether the sea could be reached by the fish, if left at such places, I was compelled to carry all which could be kept alive to the Latrobe

River, which was their original destination, and about whose ample stream I had no doubt at all.

"Throughout the journey the utmost friendliness and interest was shown by railway officials, by the *employés* of Messrs. Cobb and Co., and by all the people who were met on the road.

"Mr. Roden, to whom every turn in the road has long been familiar—who drove the first woman along it, and the first baby—himself drove the coach from the Bunyip, rendering all possible assistance, and taking pleasure in driving the first salmon to the Gippsland waters.

" I am, &c.,

" ARTHUR S. KING.

" *December 27th,* 1877."

The following account of the liberation of a portion of the salmon fry in the Wannon and Glenelg Rivers will be of interest (*Argus,* January 5) :—

" Shire of Kowree, Council-chambers, Harrow, December 27, 1877. Sir Samuel Wilson, Ercildoune. Sir,—I have the pleasure to inform you, that the consignment of salmon you so kindly placed at the disposal of the shire, were liberated in splendid condition. I left about thirty with Mr. Brayshay, at Hamilton, who had undertaken to place them in the head waters of the Wannon. On my way through Cavendish, Mr. O'Connor deposited twenty-five in the Wannon at that place. At Balmoral, Mr. Lang assisted me to distribute about 200 in various suitable spots in the Glenelg. The remainder of the fish were dispersed here and there above and below Harrow, where the arrival of the little strangers received a welcome in true Christmas style, their arrival having been anxiously waited for. A breakdown on the road near Cavendish caused many hours' delay, but thanks to the excellent apparatus supplied, and to your very lucid written instructions,

furnished me by Mr. Learmonth, I succeeded in transporting them over sixty miles of rough road, with the loss
of only three fish, one of which I found dead at Balmoral,
and two at Harrow. The last batch were placed in the
Glenelg at 8 p.m. on Christmas Day. They seemed as
lively and active as at starting from Hamilton, but appeared
ravenously hungry. A small white moth, having accidentally fallen into the water, was vigorously attacked, and
carried to the bottom of the bucket with almost lightning
rapidity, every time he floated to the surface. The next
meeting of our shire council takes place on Wednesday,
2nd prox., when I am sure the councillors will be glad to
learn the so-far success of this portion of your efforts, to
improve the piscatorial resources of the colony.—I beg to
remain, your most obedient servant, J. S. MACKENZIE,
Secretary and Engineer of Kowree Shire."

Mr. J. H. Connor, in the letter from which the following
extracts are given, furnishes some interesting details
concerning the streams near Cape Otway, in which a
portion of the salmon fry have been successfully liberated.
They were taken to Apollo Bay and Blanket Bay by the
Government steamer *Pharos*, on her way to supply the
lighthouses in that neighbourhood with stores, for which
purpose this vessel is required to go there occasionally.
He says :—

" We divided 250 of the fry into four small fish-tins of
water, reducing the temperature well with ice, and proceeded across the windings of the Burrum Burrum River
from the sea inland. . . . . We liberated the first
sixty-five fish at a point in the river about three miles
from the sea ; and I may here state that the river runs
inland from ten to fifteen miles. It is well and closely
shaded with trees of different kinds, and undergrowth.
The water is very cold and clear, running over a gravelly

bed; just the river, I believe, that will prove to be most suitable for the acclimatisation of the salmon. The young fry seemed to enjoy their new home immensely, and quickly headed up the stream, in regular marching order. We followed the course of the river for about four or five miles, and liberated 185 more of the fry (250 in all) at different places in the stream.

"The land near to the river, and fronting the bay, appeared to me to be capable of growing almost anything. Mr. Cawood's green clover paddocks are a pleasing sight in themselves at this season of the year. Altogether, I much liked the rather wild and romantic look of the country at and around Apollo Bay, and I venture to say that it will some day be a place of importance. In our absence, while liberating the fish, the crew of the *Pharos* had landed Mr. Cawood's stores, so that we were, on our return, enabled to at once proceed to Blanket Bay, where we arrived about eleven o'clock the same morning. . . We were, without delay, rowed to the shore in the large boat of the *Pharos*, and carried on shore by the sailors, when we at once divided the fish into four fish-tins, largely supplied with iced water, and rolled the tins round with rugs and canvas. Messrs. Stevenson and Walls had, at their own expense, provided pack-horses, all ready . . . and we started for the Aire River. The journey through the bush was very difficult and trying. We crossed the Parker River at about two miles inland from the sea, and took advantage of its delightfully cold and clear water to replenish our fish-tins, and we also placed the tins themselves in the stream for half an hour, at the same time liberating in the water twelve of the young fish. The reason that we did not put more in the Parker is, that the falls in it near to the sea are very steep, and the stream is very much blocked up with timber. The fish will have no difficulty in getting to the sea, but I fear they will not succeed in returning. We reached the Aire at a point near to its junction with the sea. Here Messrs. Walls and Stevenson had a boat provided, in which we rowed up the river, with the fish-tins covered with wet rags, the day being very hot. Mr. Walls recommended that we should go up the Ford River, a tributary of the Aire, which we did, and liberated sixty of the young fry in it. We then rowed up the Aire for about four or five miles, and liberated the remainder of the fish, about 175, making in all 247 in the Aire, the Ford, and the Parker rivers, only losing four fish from the total number of 500 received at Ballarat. The Aire River is twenty to thirty yards wide, about a mile and a half from the sea, and continues a good width for about two or three miles inland. It is, however, liable to be barred in certain seasons, with the sand washing in from the ocean. Only recently Messrs. Stevenson and Walls scooped out a passage, for its accumulated waters to get to the sea, and thereby considerably reduced the depth of the river, and drained a large extent of swampy land adjoining it. The scenery along the banks of the stream is beautiful to look at, but the water in the river itself is much warmer than the waters of the Parker or the Burrum Burrum. . . . Altogether, I believe that the experiment to acclimatise the salmon in these rivers will prove to be a success."

The following appeared in the *Argus* of January 19th, 1878, and is an account of my trip to Gippsland, with the salmon fry intended for distribution, in the rivers flowing from the Great Dividing Range known as the Australian Alps, some of which run direct to the sea, and others into the great lakes which receive many of the Gippsland streams, and have their embouchure by the Reeves River, through a shifting sand-bar, into the Pacific Ocean.

K

I had originally intended to have taken the fish intended for Gippsland, and more especially those for the Snowy River, by sea, and had postponed making any arrangements for stocking these rivers, until the return of the Government steamer *Victoria* from her cruise, which I understood was to terminate about Christmas. An application made by the Zoological and Acclimatisation Society to the Government, for the use of the *Victoria* to take the salmon to Gippsland, had been very favorably received, and on seeing her arrival reported in the *Argus*, I at once wrote to the Commissioner of Trade and Customs, asking that arrangements might be made as soon as convenient, to send the fish to the entrance to the Gippsland Lakes, and to the mouth of the Snowy River, and that the steam launch of the *Cerberus* might be taken, to go through the surf and ascend the Snowy River with the young salmon. Not receiving any reply in a few days, I had an interview with the Hon. Mr. Lalor, who then stated that the *Victoria* could not be sent on this trip, as there was no money to pay the officers and men, on account of the political difficulties between the two houses of Parliament, and that Captain Stanley, the commander of the *Victoria*, did not consider it safe to land near, or to enter the mouth of the Snowy River, unless in very calm weather, as the coast is unsheltered, and a dangerous surf from the Pacific Ocean, breaks upon the long stretch of the littoral line known as the Ninety-Mile Beach, near the mouth of the Snowy River. I had an interview with Captain Stanley, who pointed out the risk of being detained for days, if high winds should blow landwards on that coast, and the danger to the lives of his men, should a landing be attempted in such circumstances, and it became evident that the idea of getting the *Victoria* to transport the fish, must be abandoned.

I then applied to the Gippsland Steam Navigation Company, and with great liberality they at once offered to convey the fish free of charge by any of their steamers, to the Lakes Entrance, or to any point on their usual route. They also expressed their intention to send a small steamer soon, on an exploring expedition to the Snowy River, which could take the fish at the same time. This very liberal offer I at first intended to accept, but on enquiry I found that many days might be occupied by the trip, and the difficulty of keeping the fish alive for such a long period, together with the risk of windy weather, which might cause further delay, caused me to decide upon taking them overland.

I then applied to the Hon. Mr. Woods, the Minister of Railways, who showed every desire to assist me, and placed the whole department at my service in the most liberal manner. As it is necessary in the transit of salmon that no delay should occur, I asked for a special train to run during the night, and to go over the contractors' lines as far as practicable.

I found, on inquiring of Mr. Higinbotham, who kindly offered to assist me, that only four miles of a gap was left in the whole line from Oakleigh to Sale, the rails being laid all the rest of the way. I then applied to the contractors, asking for permission to run a Government train over their uncompleted lines, to convey the salmon fry, which request they at once and most readily granted; and not only so, but Messrs. Fishbourne and Morton, and Messrs. Noonan Brothers gave their personal attendance during the night, and furnished men to assist in carrying the cans, and also riding-horses where required. The Railway Department not having a spare engine to do the work, asked the contractors for the use of their engine on hire, which was most readily granted; and

K 2

Messrs. Fishbourne and Morton and Messrs. Noonan, with great generosity, not only carried the salmon and a large party over their own line, but Messrs. Noonan's engine went also all the way to Sale over the Government line, free of any charge to either myself or the Government.

I arranged with Messrs. Robertson and Wagner, to send an express waggon to carry the fish cans over the four miles of a gap, between the ends of the completed railway lines, and also to convey the salmon from Sale to Bairnsdale.

The conveyance of the salmon beyond this place—which is the furthest point to which Cobb's coaches run—I left to be arranged by the Bairnsdale Shire Council. However, the day before that fixed for starting, I had a telegram from the secretary to the shire, to the effect that it was "impossible" to take the salmon by the route I had indicated, and advising me to go by steamer.

I decided, however, to endeavour to carry out my original plan, and accordingly, on Thursday last, at a quarter past five p.m., I left Ercildoune with about 2,700 salmon fry, all of which were intended for distribution in the Gippsland rivers, except a small number left at Meredith in passing, which were successfully placed in the Moorabool River, by the president of the shire of Meredith and Mr. Corker.

Soon after leaving Burrumbeet, I noticed that the fry showed symptoms of being sickly, by turning on their sides, and notwithstanding every care it soon became evident that a serious loss would occur. At Lal Lal I partially changed the water in one can, which seemed to be the worst, but could not see any improvement, and a number of them were evidently dying, and my project to take a proportion of the fish to the Snowy River, seemed little likely to be realised. With every care and

attention that could be devised, and after having, as I
thought, mastered all the difficulties attending the transit
of these fish, I had the sickening feeling that I could do
nothing to prevent the loss of possibly the whole of the
lot, and that after all the trouble I had given to so many
people, I should have put them to this inconvenience
without any good result. As the night wore on I observed
a little improvement however, and those that remained
alive, showed plainly that they had recovered from whatever had sickened them. I have not been able to account
satisfactorily for this loss, but think it may have been
caused by feeding the fry immediately before starting, to
prevent the necessity of doing so in the night, and thereby
spoiling the water ; and the fish, from their increased size,
owing to their rapid growth, probably required more space
in the cans than I had given them. The motion of the
waggon immediately after their being fed, and the vibration
of the train may have sickened them. It is somewhat
curious however, that out of over twenty lots of fry, only
the two going to Gippsland should have suffered any
serious loss, and that it should have occurred between
Burrumbeet and Melbourne in both cases.

On arriving at Melbourne, Mr. Le Souef was waiting
with Messrs. Robertson and Wagner's express waggon,
and a spring van (carrying two boxes of ice), to convey the
fish to Oakleigh railway station. An express train was
waiting there on our arrival, and soon we were on our
way at a good rate of speed. On arriving at Buneep,
Messrs. Fishbourne and Mortons's engine was attached
to the van containing the fish, and we sped on through the
forest in the darkness.

Mr. Le Souef was desirous of going through to the
Snowy, but owing to the roads being bad, I thought it
better not to have too large a party. Mr. O'Brien, of

Swan Reach, had joined the train at Oakleigh, and most kindly offered to drive me through to my destination in his buggy, with three good horses. This offer I gladly accepted, as in case of accident to the express waggon, it provided a means of saving the fish. Besides his being a most capital whip over very bad roads, his pleasant companionship made the journey a very agreeable one.

We arrived at the end of the rails without accident, although, from the line being unfenced, and from there being facing points of sidings in various places, and also from the fact of the clearing being insufficient, there was really some danger in running at the rate of forty miles an hour, under the circumstances. The trees along the line are high enough to reach—should any fall—not only the rails, but also across the line so as to touch the trees on the other side, and unless a much wider space is cleared, accidents must occur during high winds, from fallen trees obstructing the trains.

The lamps of the express waggon, driven by Mr. Roden, appeared in a few minutes after we reached the unfinished portion, and soon the fish cans, ice, &c., were transferred to his charge. And here I would express my sense of Messrs. Robertson and Wagner's generosity and public spirit, in not only giving the gratuitous use of their horses and coaches, but in the care and trouble they took to send out their road inspector, Mr. Roden, to find a practicable route, and to drive the salmon over this very difficult portion. To get his waggon there, it had to be carried some distance, and lifted over logs and stumps three feet high.

The first peep of dawn appeared in the east as we left the railway, and the increasing light helped us over the difficulties of the way. More than once the vehicle was on a balance, with two wheels in the air, but willing

hands were ready to prevent an upset, by holding on to
the waggon, and pushing it up the steep ascents that had
to be surmounted.   Mr. Fishbourne accompanied us, and
we all went on foot, but he kindly insisted on my taking
his horse, which he got out of his stable in passing.   After
some heavy work in getting through the forest, and along
the railway line, we reached the Little Moe, and on ascertaining that the water was good, by tasting it, I examined
the cans, and changed the water in those in which there
were dead fish.   We could then see the smoke of the other
train at a distance, near the end of Messrs. Noonan's
contract, and coming up to meet us.

I poured out the water through a small net, which
detained the fish, and the living ones drafted themselves
out very speedily, by leaping off the net into a can ready
placed to receive them.   On the dead fish being counted,
there were about 950, leaving between 1600 and 1700 fish
which were lively and well.   From this point onward, all
the way to the Snowy River, only four fish died out of the
number left, being a much better result than I had
expected, and although they were much fewer than I
wished to send, there were still enough to stock the rivers
they were intended for, in a way to give the experiment a
fair trial.

It was sunrise when we again started, and although the
engine seemed near, it took a long time to get up to it,
owing to the bad roads; and the waggon was at last forced
to stop, the fish-cans, ice, &c., being carried about half a
mile to the railway.   A party had come out by the train
from the Moe to meet the salmon, and although the hands
of some were more used to the pen, than to carrying
burdens, by their willing assistance we got the fish safely
into the Government van attached to Messrs. Noonan's
engine, and steamed away at a rate of speed that

promised an early arrival at Sale. The train for Melbourne was to start at eight o'clock, and the stationmaster at the Moe telegraphed to delay it fifteen minutes, till the arrival of the express. However, the powerful engine we had dashed along at such a good rate, that we were in Sale at twenty-five minutes to eight o'clock, and on reaching the station, I was received by the Mayor and Council of Sale, and the secretary and councillors of the shire of Avon; and three hearty cheers were given in honour of the event, by those assembled on the platform.

According to arrangement, vehicles were in waiting to convey the salmon. Some 250 went to the Avon River, in charge of Messrs. Little, Lloyd, and Bolden, and the mayor of Sale, with Dr. Macdonald and Messrs. Bushe and Topping, started with 250 more for the Macalister River. Without delay, after leaving written instructions how to act, a start was made with the remainder for Bairnsdale, some forty-two miles off. The fish stood the journey well, being attended to every fifteen minutes, by forcing in fresh air, and ice being used, as required, to maintain a temperature of 55 deg. The thermometer, unfortunately, got broken here, but another was provided at Bairnsdale. The weather became very hot during this part of the journey.

At Bairnsdale, Mr. Howitt, P.M., and Mr. Goold, the president of the shire, were waiting to receive us. The former volunteered to accompany us on horseback to the Snowy River, and, from his thorough acquaintance with the district during the many years he has spent there, no one could better act as guide. A more pleasant companion I would not desire to travel with, and his readiness of resource in an emergency, is invaluable in an expedition over such rough country as we had to travel through. It will be remembered that Mr. Howitt went as leader of the relief party sent to learn the fate of the ill-starred expedition of Burke and Wills, and that he accomplished the object of his mission most successfully. His son Charlton, a fine active lad of thirteen, also rode with us, and rendered good service on many occasions.

The Mitchell River flows close past Bairnsdale, and enters Lake King some miles below that place. Being desirous of knowing the temperature of its waters, while counting over the fish intended for it, I asked Mr. Goold to ascertain the surface and bottom temperature of the river. He reported 75 deg. at the surface, and 74 deg. at eleven feet deep. At the time I thought there must be some mistake, but afterwards I had good reason to know that it was quite correct, and a very much higher temperature than I could have desired for the salmon. Without delay, the waggon provided by the shire for conveyance of the fish, started for Bruthen, on the River Tambo, and as Bovill, who had come from Ercildoune in attendance on the fish, seemed quite exhausted by want of sleep, I left him behind, to wait my return, and went in the waggon to look after my charge. This duty is very light, but constant. The temperature must be regulated by ice supplied at intervals, and air must be forced into the water by bellows every fifteen minutes. Mr. O'Brien remained to get some fresh horses, and to feed those he brought on, and, after some time, he and Mr. Howitt and Charlton overtook us; and Bovill, not liking to be left behind, and feeling stronger after dinner, had come on also.

We had now left the plain country, where, at intervals, splendid wheat crops, and well-grassed paddocks, with most substantial fences, and stocked with fine cattle, showed the wealth of Gippsland; and we entered the interminable forest of the mountain slopes, facing seaward, which extends, without a break, all the way to the New South Wales boundary.

We stopped at the Nicholson, a fine stream, shaded over by wattles and gums, and running briskly over gravelly fords, into long reaches of deep water. The temperature of the water was here 72 deg. After bringing up the water by degrees from 55 deg. to about 70 deg., to prevent too sudden a shock to the salmon, we liberated a few at a place, in sheltered parts of the current, and in shallow water. There were plenty of young fish in the stream, smaller than the salmon parrs, which proved that there was a good chance for them. The high temperature did not seem to inconvenience the salmon, which headed upstream, and darted about, evidently enjoying the change.

The roads became much more difficult to go over, being through a dense forest, and across deep gullies and high ranges, timbered with a number of different kinds of Eucalypti, a variety of Banksia, and a Casuarina new to me, and an undergrowth of wattles, dogwood, &c. We arrived at Bruthen about six o'clock.

The Tambo runs past this place, which is most picturesquely situated, and is surrounded by an amphitheatre of mountain ranges, which seem quite near, and the river winds through alluvial flats, of moderate extent, but of magnificent soil, as the fine crops show very clearly. I expected to have found the water of this river much colder than that of the Mitchell, as we were so much nearer the mountains, but on reaching the stream, I found, to my surprise, that it was 75 deg. The water was running swiftly, with a murmuring sound, over a beautiful bed of clean gravel, and was clear, and pleasant to the taste, the stream being sixty yards wide. Two hundred were liberated in the fords here, and they found shelter amongst the gravel from the strong current, which carried them downwards.

The road beyond Bruthen towards the Snowy River is bad to travel over by daylight, but much worse by night,

and Mr. Howitt advised that we should remain at Bruthen
till dawn, and take some rest.

I had prepared a box for a portion of the ice, with perforated zinc inserted in the ends, and which was now
nearly empty of ice. We sank this amongst the gravel in
the current, and, after equalising the temperature, poured
the salmon and the water which they were in, out of the
cans into the box. The fish evidently enjoyed the change
from being in the cans, to a rapid current in a natural
stream, and leaped high out of the water in a way I never
saw them do before. One got over the box, jumping over
six inches high, and swam quickly away, and many leaped
much higher, but fell back again. The box was fitted with
a close lid, which prevented risk of loss in the night. The
current, being strong, carried the fish against the perforated zinc, and kept them there. To lessen the current
a wall of loose stones was built round the box, and some
placed on the top of it. The fish were fed with grated
liver, the lid closed, a rope was tied round it, and fastened
to the wheel of the waggon, to prevent its being carried
away by a sudden rise in the river; and after doing justice to our dinner, we retired to very comfortable quarters,
with the understanding that we should start at the first
peep of dawn.

Early as I was next morning, I found Mr. Howitt and
Charlton before me at the river, in the grey dawn. They
had examined the fish, and were just returning to tell me
that they were as lively as possible, except two that had
got pinned against the zinc by the force of the current,
and which were suffocated. I had been very anxious
during the night, as I did not anticipate these high temperatures, and I kept waking up, thinking of the salmon.
The test was a very severe one. These fish had never
before experienced higher temperatures than 60 deg. to

62 deg., and were out of iced water at 55 deg., besides being very young and tender. Should any large portion of them be found to have perished from the heat, it would be of little use going further, and the experiment must fail. The news brought by Charlton set my fears at rest ; success now seemed certain, and soon we were on our road to the Buchan, the nearest tributary of the Snowy River.

The road became more difficult as we advanced, deep gullies, with bad crossing-places, alternated with steep hills and bad sidlings. It was found necessary to tie up one or two wheels in going down the precipitous slopes, and occasionally all hands assisted in getting the waggon, with the load, up the steep ascent of some range. A spring was found to be broken in the express waggon, and we stopped to repair it as well as we could, and lessened the quantity of water in the fish cans, to lighten the load.

On starting again, a splinter-bar of Mr. O'Brien's buggy broke, in making the ascent out of Stony Creek. The waggon was not delayed, and by the aid of a sapling, some rope, and Mr. Howitt's skill as a bushman, we were soon on the way again.

It was thought at first that if the fry were put into the Buchan, a tributary of the Snowy, that they would find their way there in time, and so accomplish the desired object, but I felt that my undertaking would be incomplete, if I did not get a portion of them placed in the Snowy River. On inquiring we obtained Mr. Mackieson as guide, who promised to conduct us by a near way, but a bad road, to the Snowy River, near to its junction with the Buchan.

Two bullock teams were camped on the road, and the drivers were sitting smoking on a log after eating their dinner. As we passed them Bovill got the bellows and tube and commenced blowing into the cans. One bullock-

driver started to his feet with a face of astonishment, and
an untranslatable exclamation. I fancy we must have
been taken by him for a party of escaped lunatics, come
over the mountains from the Beechworth Asylum. Both
men stood looking after us till lost to sight in the windings
of the road. The incident afforded us a good hearty laugh
for some time after.

We came to the Tara Creek, on the watershed of the
Snowy—a beautiful small stream of water clear as crystal.
It did not taste well however, and I could not see a single
fish after examining it for a long distance, and did not
liberate any fish there. After a very rough road, we at
last arrived at a hill close to the Buchan River, and from
this point the fish were carried on horseback, in small cans,
over very precipitous country, and 200 were liberated in
the Buchan, a beautiful stream of good clear water, with
gravelly beds, and with small fish in shoals. Our horses
were led, and slid down the sandy bank into the stream, on
their haunches. Only a high hill now separated us from
the valley of the Snowy River.

On ascending the slope, our guide had the can with the
fish (about 400) before him on the saddle, and I rode close
behind. Suddenly the sandy bank gave way, just as he
had surmounted the last ascent, and horse, rider, and fish-
can were rolling in the sand. I dismounted in a moment,
and ran to save the fish, expecting to see them scattered
about on the sand, but although the water had partially
escaped, none of the fish were lost, as the perforated top
of the can was fastened with a hasp. Thus within the last
mile, the object of our journey was nearly being frustrated.
I carried the fish the remainder of the way.

On arriving at the top of the ridge the Snowy River
lay at our feet, but it looked muddy and turbid, as if in
flood from recent rains in the hills. It has every indication

of being a rapid mountain stream, subject to heavy floods, which are said to rise sixty feet in a night. There is an island of boulders and waterworn pebbles at its junction with the Buchan of some thirty acres, completely denuded of soil, by the strength of the current. Not liking to put the fish in the muddy water, I carried them to the junction, and wading through the Buchan, I liberated them some distance below the junction, but in the clear water of the Buchan, which did not intermingle for a considerable distance with the muddy waters of the Snowy River—just as is seen at the confluence of the Rhone and the Arve, near Geneva, where the blue waters of the lake unite, but do not mingle with, the muddy waters brought down by the melted snows from Chamounix. I got rather chaffed for wading into the water unnecessarily, but wet clothes did not seem of much consequence at the moment, and the strong heat of the weather soon dried them.

Mr. Howitt went to make some geological examinations of the pebble and boulder drift, which contained specimens of many varieties of rocks, all rounded and waterworn ; even large blocks of over two feet in diameter had apparently been rolled down by the force of the current in times of flood. The channel of the Snowy river is probably 300 feet to 400 feet wide, and near its confluence with the Buchan runs between high steep ranges. It is more than twice the width, and has three or four times the volume of the Yarra, and runs swiftly over pebbly shoals and rocky rapids. It is said to be often muddy from rains in the hills, but is generally bright and clear. There is a waterfall about twenty-five miles above the junction, about twelve feet high, but it is not an abrupt descent, and salmon could ascend it easily. There is no other barrier that I could hear of. It is well stocked with fish of good quality. The temperature of its water, to my surprise, was 73½ deg.   Higher up the river, no doubt, it is much cooler, and I wished greatly that the salmon could have been first taken there.   The Buchan was half a degree warmer, or 74 deg., and this stream seemed to me better suited to salmon than the Snowy, although they will, in my opinion, do well in both rivers.   It has been stated that the Californian salmon goes through waters in its native country up to a temperature of 85 deg. in safety.   In the Avon the fry perished at 83 deg.   In a brisk current they will live at temperatures that they could not bear in still water, and in all the Gippsland rivers a good stream runs throughout the driest summer.   The present season has been exceptionally dry and hot, and my journey took place a few days after mid-summer, in the very hottest season of the year.

After having a short rest and a pot of tea, we retraced our steps and patched up the damaged buggy, pushing along rapidly, and at about ten o'clock on Saturday night reached Gibb's at Stony Creek, and next day Bairnsdale, where I parted with regret from Mr. Howitt and his son, and Mr. O'Brien.   The buggy broke down completely, and was brought on by a bullock-dray.   As Parliament was to meet on Tuesday I was obliged to travel through the night, to catch the train at Sale at eight o'clock on Monday morning, and arrived in Melbourne about ten o'clock on Monday, having travelled about 600 miles, over the worst roads in the colony, in a wonderfully short time.

I cannot close this account of my trip without mention of George Witts, the driver of the waggon from Bairnsdale to the Snowy River, to whose care and skill the safety of the fish is greatly due, and of Mr. Mackieson's services as guide, which were of great value in shortening the journey.   The Shire of Bairnsdale had liberally provided for the conveyance of the fish.

I would especially refer to the liberality of Mr. C. Umphelby, on behalf of the directors of the Ice Company, who supplied, free of charge, all the ice required for more than fifteen different trips. On this, as on many previous occasions, the Victoria Ice Company has rendered good service to the cause of acclimatisation, for which they deserve the thanks of the community.

The Minister of Railways most freely gave every assistance in his power, and the ice, the fish-cans, and an attendant, were allowed to travel free in all cases, and three special trains were provided for the Gippsland road.

But for the great interest taken in the experiment by all engaged in it, the same amount of success could not have been attained. The fish were watched over by Philip Smith from the earliest stage, with a care and assiduity that could not be excelled. In my Gellibrand trip Mr. Gordon Gardner drove the waggon through the night, over a road that would have alarmed a less fearless driver. Mr. Le Souef was always ready to give a helping hand, at all hours of the day and night, and now it only remains for Nature to do her part to have in a few years, should fortune favour the experiment (as it has hitherto done in a most remarkable manner), results which will provide a new sport to make the colony more attractive, and a new source of profit, from the rivers and seas of this portion of our island continent.

The rivers and streams in which the salmon have been placed, include all streams of any note extending into South Australia on one side, and into New South Wales on the other. Including two or three small lots yet to distribute, the rivers included in the experiment are the Glenelg, at three places 100 miles apart; Darlot's Creek, near Portland: the Hopkins, the Fiery Creek, Lake Burrumbeet, and Emu Creek; the Gellibrand and tribu-

taries, the Erskine, St. George, and Cumberland, at Loutitt
Bay ; the Aire, Barrum, Ford, and Parker, at Cape Otway ;
the Barwon, at Winchelsea and Birregurra ; the Werribee,
the Saltwater River, the Yarra, the Latrobe, the Macalister,
the Avon, the Mitchell, the Nicholson, the Tambo, and the
Snowy Rivers.

It is important to know that the salmon have been
placed in streams that afford a good promise of successful
results. The Cape Otway streams are all highly spoken
of by those who know them, as being most suitable. The
Aire River about six miles west of Cape Otway, has a wide
estuary into which flow three tributaries from a tract of
country of a semi-alpine character. There are extensive
forests of the beautiful evergreen beech (*Fagus Cunning-
hami*), many of the trees being splendid specimens from
four to five feet in diameter. There are many beautiful
spots in these ranges near the base of Mount Sabine,
waterfalls and rapids, with fern trees fifty feet in height.

Near Loutitt Bay there are clear, cool streams, with
pebbly bottoms coming direct out of high ranges. Mr.
Edward Hayes, who carried some of the salmon fry on
pack horses over almost inaccessible country and liberated
them successfully, speaks highly in praise of these streams
as being most suitable for salmon.

The Gippsland rivers are splendid streams, which never
fail in the driest seasons. The Avon is described by
Mr. Bolden as one of the best streams flowing into the
Lakes. Its tributaries are most suitable for fish-spawning,
being extremely clear, with a rocky and pebbly bottom.

The Mitchell, and its principal tributaries, the Dargo,
Wentworth, Wonnongatta, and Morocco, take their rise
from the great dividing range, and receive the drainage from
the melting snows of a watershed having a very large area.

Mining operations having now all but ceased on these

L

streams, their waters are bright, clear, cold, and rapid, and they are stated by Mr. Bredt, the engineer to the shire of Bairnsdale, to be free from all enemies to the young salmon.

One thousand salmon fry were sent to the Hopkins river near Warrnambool, by sea, and were taken there by Mr. Hickling.   In his report he says:—" I got down with the fish very successfully, and liberated them in excellent condition in the Cudgee Creek.   I am sure they will do well, as the temperature (on 27th December) was only 57 deg., and—dry as it is—there is now a splendid stream of the purest water.   The temperature of the Hopkins was 64 deg.—no doubt cooler in the shady pools and shallows—but this was after the great heat of Saturday ; however, the fish did not appear to be at all inconvenienced by the change from the cool tank to the warmer river.   I am confident they will be heard of again."

In distributing the young salmon it was not found convenient to delay the fish so as to count carefully the large number sent off at once—in one case eight thousand ; but the number was estimated approximately by counting out one hundred into a bucket, and afterwards netting about the same number as near as could be guessed, and noting the number of hundreds put in the cans.   The later lots, being smaller in number, were counted with care, and, when all were counted, a very considerable loss was found to have unaccountably taken place, but it was found that lizards and snakes had made their way into one of the hatching boxes, and no doubt they had devoured many of the *alevins*.   One snake was caught inside of the cover of wire netting put over the hatching-race, and killed, and a lizard was found with a *galaxias* five inches long, which it had dragged out of the water, and which was still alive.

An objection has been made to my dividing the salmon into different lots, as it is supposed that they would have had a better prospect of success if a large number had been placed in one river. From the fact of six pairs of breeding trout having only been retained in the ponds at New Norfolk, and that these, with thirty more turned into the river, are the parents of all the trout in these colonies, it will be evident that by dividing the salmon the chances of success are greatly increased. It is impossible to tell which river may prove best suited to them, but when all the rivers in the colony of any note, have been tried, if at all suitable to the climate, they must succeed in some of them, and I had so many applications for a portion of the fish, that I could not well refuse to send a few to each river.

Even from Tasmania I had a request for a few of the fry to put in the Mersey, and sent off 200 there, but from some cause, which I could not ascertain (possibly *mal-de-mer*) all but seven fish perished during the sea-voyage, and these, I fear, will never be heard of again, although they were safely liberated in that fine stream, the Mersey River. I hope that my Tasmanian friends will be more fortunate the next time that a similar attempt is made.

I would here express my grateful appreciation of the warm interest in the undertaking shown by the public and the Press, but especially by the *Argus*, while the experiment was in progress. I also had very kind, and, indeed, in some cases, far too flattering expressions of acknowledgment from Shire Councils and from Angling Societies, and a most kind recognition of my exertions by the Council of the Zoological and Acclimatisation Society. And to one and all I would offer my most hearty thanks for the kind feeling shown in connection with my undertaking, which has been so far successful, thanks to the good fortune which, under the blessing of Divine Providence, has attended the experiment, and to the able assistance that many have so freely rendered to promote that result.

REPORT

ON THE

SOCIETY'S OSTRICHES,

NOW RUNNING ON

MESSRS. OFFICER BROS.' STATION, MURRAY DOWNS,

BY

S. H. OFFICER, Esq.

———————

THE Members of the Society may be somewhat disappointed at the result of the long attempt to acclimatise the ostrich and to render its introduction into the colony a source of profit to themselves as well as a very important addition to the national resources of this great continent. But when all the circumstances attending the experiment are considered (for after all the attempt must still be deemed only on trial in this latitude) it will not be surprising that greater things have not been achieved, and that the glowing anticipations of large returns from the produce of the birds and the augmentation of their numbers, has not yet been quite realised.

From the experience of the past, however, the Society may now at length well indulge in fresh hope and look forward at no very distant date to securing a more tangible and practical result than a mere report and hope of better things to come has hitherto afforded them. In transporting the birds from the Wimmera to the Murray great loss was unfortunately sustained. During the journey a week of one of the heaviest rains which has ever occurred in Victoria overtook them ; the waggons conveying them were delayed, and the last week on the road proved fatal to several. Of the three hen birds which safely arrived here, one unfortunately escaped from the enclosure they were placed in, through the negligence of a workman employed about them in leaving a gate open, and immediately after the bird, running into a wire fence, was killed upon the spot.

Another, the only tame bird of the flock, was old and worn out, and died after laying her first and only egg. The third hen, the only one left from which to rear a flock, and upon which all the hopes of ultimate success now solely depended, was fortunately strong and healthy, and from this bird alone has been raised the present promising little flock.

On their first arrival at Murray Downs the birds were extremely wild (excepting only the old hen), and could not be approached in the large yard in which they were kept without evidencing great fear, and rushing violently about the enclosure. By perseverance, constantly seeing people, and daily feeding, this timidity at length quite disappeared, and as soon as practicable they were removed into a secure and properly sheltered paddock, of suitable size, and specially erected for them, and the daily feeding and watering continued the same as previously in the smaller enclosure.

Early in the summer the hen bird laid her first nest of eggs, and as we had by this time obtained from the Cape a patent Douglass Incubator, at a cost of about £100, it was determined to try the eggs in this instead of leaving them to the natural process, where the risk of losing all from so many outside causes was so great.

The immediate result of this novel process promised well, and a good many young birds were hatched But unfortunately, one by one the growing chicks were attacked by the disease which proves so fatal at the Cape, and which has here hitherto, as will be seen, also been the main obstacle in the successful breeding of this valuable and interesting bird.

The young chick exhibits the first symptoms of illness by appearing unsteady on its feet, and this gradually increases until at length it is unable to stand still, and must keep moving rapidly about, or fall to the ground. The appetite all the time and until near the end remains as good as ever. At length the bird, worn to a skeleton by constant running, is unable to rise, and death then soon follows.

At the Cape the disease is said to be blood poisoning, and is thought to be a result of too close herding and housing at night, and, these causes being avoided as far as possible, they now suffer but little. Here it has proved even more fatal and difficult to deal with, for the young birds have fallen victims to it although reared entirely by their mothers and kept in an open paddock.

On the Wimmera, too, under Sir Samuel (then Mr.) Wilson's care, where the birds were not confined at all, we believe the disease was equally, if not more, destructive.

In nearly every case here the bird has died after being once attacked, and in not a single instance has recovered its proper health. Two of the flock now afflicted with the disease for nearly eighteen months have not lately appeared any worse, and are even becoming a little steadier on their legs, and gaining better condition of body, though very much undersized ; but complete recovery cannot be expected, though they may live and hobble about in their peculiar manner for years to come.

If they remain free from attack for the first year, they, as far as our experience has gone, escape altogether. An examination of several after death showed the feet and legs to be extensively congested, but all the vital organs were quite healthy.

A second attempt was made with the incubator during the following winter, when the hen, in a most unaccountable manner, began laying. To have left the bird to hatch these eggs herself could only have been useless in result, as the cold and wet days at that season would have at once destroyed the delicate young chicks, which are so extremely sensitive to these causes, and no other alternative was therefore open for dealing with the eggs. The process at first promised excellent results, and great hopes were entertained of a large increase to the flock, but once more disappointment ensued. Of the chicks safely hatched all fell victims to the disease before referred to, until at length, after six or eight months, only two out of all the flock remained alive, and these soon after died.

The next eggs were laid in the following summer, and were left entirely to the parent birds to hatch, but some of the chicks having died soon after birth from the effects of a heavy thunderstorm, and the rest being in danger from other causes—chief among which was that arising from the attacks of the cock birds, who would speedily have killed them all—it was deemed advisable to place them in charge of a keeper. This was accordingly done, and the final result of this hatching was six birds, four of which are healthy and two diseased. These are now nearly old enough for breeding, and the former, or healthy ones, show signs of a desire to pair.

This lot of birds possess the immense advantage of being perfectly tame and easily driven or enticed wherever desired, which the older birds can not be without considerable forcing and then only within secure fences. They are quite domesticated, and will eat freely from the hand of any one entering their enclosure.

The hen having again laid a nest of eggs, and brought out six chicks late in the autumn, in consequence of the very mild and dry winter of last year, they were successfully reared through the delicate stage of their growth, and having quite escaped the usual disease, have now grown into large birds, and promise as well as any of the whole flock. They are, however, rather wild, and can only be closely approached by their keeper.

During last summer the old hen once more laid and brought out a clutch of young birds. These were not taken from her, but though very carefully attended to, fed, and watched, the result has been unsatisfactory. Two or three were carried off by an eagle during the dinner hour, and when they were about as large as their assailant itself. No danger from this source had been suspected, and it was only when the last chick was taken that the cause of the mysterious disappearance of the others was made plain. The eagle was shot by the keeper while in the act of carrying off the body of the young bird. The male ostrich killed two others, and the rest that died were taken off by the common disease. Three now only remain, and one of these is already ill, though not of late getting any worse. If no further casualties arise with the young birds now nearly full grown, next summer, or at the latest the one following, should see at least five or six hen birds in full laying condition, and these, with the great attention they receive and the fuller experience regarding their management which has now been gained, should speedily expand into a large and profitable flock of ostriches.

The number and description of the flock as it now exists is as follows :—

3 old cocks

1 old hen

6 birds, about 20 months old, classed thus—
 4 healthy— 2 males, 2 females
 2 diseased—1 male, 1 female

6 birds, about 15 months old, all healthy—
 4 males, 2 females

3 birds, about 7 months old, classed thus—
 2 healthy, females apparently
 1 diseased, female apparently

19 Total.

The process of hatching the eggs and rearing the young chicks by the old birds themselves, entirely destroys the large and delicate white feathers, which in the tail and wings of the cock, at another time and in his natural condition, unfettered by the restraints of man, are so perfect and graceful. After the sitting these feathers are useless for purposes of sale, and the parent birds, as far as the production of feathers is concerned, are a source of no profit.

The period of incubation we have found to vary from 30 to 35 days in eggs placed under the birds themselves, and in the incubator from 40 to 45 days. Whence this immense variation arises we are unable to say, but it is often a source of no small difficulty in dealing with the young chicks as they come out. The parent birds sit alternately on the eggs and watch over them with the most assiduous care, never leaving them for more than a very few minutes uncovered. In general, as soon as one rises from the nest the other at once takes its place, and sometimes both may be seen sitting together.

The first egg is laid on the bare ground without any apparent previous selection of site or attempt at preparing a nest, but just dropped on the spot the bird happens to be in when the first inclination to lay comes upon her. By degrees, as the eggs increase, the place gets worn and gradually becomes hollowed out, and presents finally the appearance of a formed nest. During incubation, and after the young birds are hatched, the male ostrich becomes very savage and will furiously attack any man or animal approaching near enough to him. He spreads out his wings, and these, with the white feathers tipping the ends and adorning the tail, he quivers rapidly to and fro, and then, with the jet black body mounted on its long legs, and the head with its immense brilliant eyes for a centre-piece, he walks slowly towards the foe, uttering a low and deep guttural sound. On approaching near enough his excitement and motions rapidly increase ; he extends his long neck, opens his mouth, shakes his wings rapidly up and down and presents an appearance enough to terrify any living animal. He finally makes a rush at his opponent, and if the latter has not before this taken to his heels and escaped to the fence he has not a further moment to lose, and woe betide the man or dog that this ostrich overtakes and strikes with his powerful foot or sharp pointed toe. A broken limb, with torn clothes and a lacerated body would be the smallest effect of the onset. At other seasons the birds may generally be safely approached.

Hitherto the birds, so far from being profitable to us, have been the source of a large annual expenditure, without any equivalent return, and it is only the firm belief of being eventually successful with this novel industry, and rendering thus a permanent benefit to the country, as well as remunerating the society and ourselves for all the past loss of time and expense, that induces us still to persevere and endeavour to extend the flock.

With regard to the most important object of rearing the ostrich, the production of a profitable yield of feathers, not much has yet been accomplished, beyond that which, like the rearing of the chicks, affords us satisfactory grounds for anticipating the happiest results in the future.

The first plucking we made, being the produce of birds confined to scarce half an acre of ground, and being torn, dirty, ragged, and badly grown, was considered useless for trade, and being offered in Melbourne realised nothing. The next, taken from the birds after they had quite recovered their clean appearance, and though scarcely up to the quality that we expect for the future was a more successful sale, and being sent to London for disposal *netted* a sum of £26, and was pronounced a parcel superior to any of the Cape birds, and equal to the feathers of the wild ones. The third plucking, taken only from two cocks that had not been running with the hens, was of excellent quality, but this has not yet been realised.

The manner of taking the feathers is simple and easily accomplished. We have a strong and secure yard in which the birds for operating upon are daily fed, and are therefore well accustomed to. Into this they are enticed. At one side is a crush panel, carefully lined with prepared boards placed a few inches apart, wide enough to admit the hand. A single bird is driven into this, and the door securely closed behind, leaving the ostrich in a space only large enough to hold his body, and affording no room for turning or struggling. The hand is then inserted between the boards at the side and the feathers carefully pulled out as desired. No injury whatever is done to the bird beyond the fright sustained and a little ruffling of the small feathers, with, at the worst, a scratch or two on the lower part of the leg.

It has been found by growers at the Cape that the *plucking* of the feathers permanently interferes with the growth of the ensuing crop, decreasing the quantity and injuring the quality, and that eventually many of the birds become utterly useless except for breeding purposes; and we have now before us an extract from the letter of a well-known ostrich farmer at the Cape published in the *Graaf Reinet Advertiser*, in which he says, "I most certainly advocate the clipping of feathers at seven months, after the stumps have been pulled out. When I have clipped the feathers I leave the stumps in for four months until they are thoroughly ripe, which brings the stump to eleven months, when it will be found to come out quite easy, without hurting the birds. In fact some of them are then already falling out." He also says, "In the pulling process the holes get filled up with congealed blood, and the succeeding crop of feathers having to find its way through a socket of the wing with hard blood in it, is much injured." And "I have bought birds that I knew to have been pulled every six months. But buying them for breeding purposes I was not particular as to their being spoilt. I knew them to have been good birds. They were utterly spoilt. One hen for three years only yielded four or five feathers in each wing. The rest were mere little sinews. The one cock bird had about ten feathers, nor did he produce any more for a full year. These birds I left in their breeding camps, and after waiting as above the feathers started. I pursued my plan of clipping and they now yield me as good a crop of feathers as could be wished." "From this it seems pretty certain that not only is the clipping process less cruel than that of pulling, but in the end is more conducive to the well-being and productiveness of the bird. This being so, we can hardly believe that ostrich farmers generally will continue a practice that is in itself cruel, and which is contrary to their own best interests. The Royal Humane Society of England has, we believe, had the matter under its consideration, and we trust the general adoption of the system pursued by Mr. Meintjes will put a stop to the charges of cruelty so frequently brought against South African ostrich farmers."—*Advertiser*.

This process we therefore propose in future to adopt, not only from motives of pecuniary advantage, but from feelings of humanity.

The birds we now have are enclosed in four substantial paddocks, one of the last erected being of three rails and prepared for short palings all round, as a security for the young birds after they are hatched, and varying in size from forty to ten acres, selected in places for purposes of security, shelter and dryness of soil, and as the numbers of the birds increase more must be added. It is a question whether we shall not once more adopt the use of the incubator; for if the disease to which the young birds are so liable could only be avoided, there is no doubt of the immense advantages the artificial hatching has over the natural process; but before any further experiment can be made, we must have a larger flock to operate with.

They require constant supervision, and one man is employed at nothing else than attending to them, with occasional help as may be required. They are daily fed with chopped lucerne, which we grow on irrigated ground, or other green food, sorghum, and maize, besides having a regular supply of crushed bones and small gravel, as well as abundance of natural herbage and grass in their separate enclosures. They are consequently always in prime condition, and this is an essential to the proper growth of the feathers and to their successful breeding.

They have also our own personal attention, and nothing that care and expenditure can accomplish has been spared to bring about a successful issue to this laudable and patriotic attempt of the Society to acclimatise the bird, and to render its introduction into Australia a source of national industry and wealth.

From the severe droughts to which this continent is so frequently liable, and from the heavy stocking with sheep and cattle to which it is in general subjected, irrespective of the natural and *unnatural* enemies in the form of man with his advancing civilization, with which it would have to contend, we think it would be quite impossible ever to acclimatise the ostrich here in a wild condition, even if such an attempt should be thought desirable.

OFFICER BRS.

Murray Downs, 14*th June*, 1878.

The following Paper on the Chinese Yam, and its culti-
vation, was read by Sir Samuel Wilson, before the Council
of the Zoological and Acclimatisation Society, at its Fort-
nightly Meeting of the 3rd June, 1878. A unanimous vote
of thanks was accorded to the writer.

THE CHINESE YAM.

Although the Chinese yam has been introduced into
this colony for a considerable time, it has not been appre-
ciated as its merits deserve. It has been hitherto cultivated more as a curiosity, than as a valuable esculent, and
it is my belief that, if properly known, it would come into
general use, as an important addition to the list of vegetables in daily use at our tables. It is a most excellent
tuber, somewhat similar to the common potato, but of a
snowy whiteness, and of a delicious flaky consistency, far
surpassing the potato in flavour.

It is known scientifically as the *Dioscorea Japonica* of
Thunberg, or the *Dioscorea batatas* of Decaisne, having
been named after Dioscorides, a Greek physician, and is
extensively cultivated in China and through a great part
of the East, as well as in Fiji and the South Sea Islands,
where it, or a nearly allied species, forms a large part of
the food of the natives at certain seasons of the year.
Thunberg, a celebrated botanist, and a disciple of Linnæus,
discovered the *Dioscorea Japonica* towards the end of the
last century, and it was introduced into Victoria by Baron
von Mueller in 1858.

M

Its cultivation is easy, and it is very prolific, yielding not only underground tubers, but also small aerial tubers in the axils of the leaf-stalks, which serve as sets for planting, to produce a crop of tubers, suitable for sets for the succeeding year's crop.

It thrives best in loamy or sandy soil of a deep and rich nature, but it succeeds well in any good soil, which, if deeply trenched and well manured, produces tubers of an astonishing size.

The roots, or tubers, are fusiform, and in shape something like a carrot or parsnip, but with this difference, that the large end grows downwards; and they are of great length, being usually from eighteen inches to two feet long, and tapering from two inches in diameter to about half an inch, in tubers of the size which are most convenient for use. It is a peculiarity of the plant, however, that the produce is in proportion to the size of the set planted, and by using large sets, tubers of over a hundred pounds can, under favourable circumstances of soil and climate, be produced. The Chinese yam is a climber, and it does best when there is something for the runners to twine round, such as a few rods or a wire stretched along the row; the reason being that the young shoots are very brittle and tender, and they are liable to be damaged by the wind blowing them about, and injuring the top buds of the runners. The best sets to plant are the small ends of the tubers, about six to nine inches long, with the small end uppermost, the bud coming from that part first, and most readily. As this portion of the tuber is too small for the table, it is usually saved for planting. Any fragment of the tuber will, however, form a plant, as there are dormant eyes all over its surface, from which buds will proceed. When the ground is cleaned, manured, and prepared, the sets should be planted in ridges eighteen inches apart, in a sloping posi-

tion, and a convenient way of doing this is to make a sloping
hole with an iron bar, and place the set in it, with the small
end about two inches below the surface, the sets being six
inches apart in the rows. The reason of their doing best
when planted sloping, is that the new root is not then liable
to be injured by the old one decaying. There is usually
but one tuber to each plant, although there may be two
or three, if anything interferes with the downward progress
of the first root formed. If a small tuber or set be planted,
a much larger one will be produced. If a large one be
planted whole, one much larger still will be the result, the
set decaying away, or becoming shrivelled as the plant is
developed, as in the common potato.

The ærial tubers, which are globular in shape, vary in
size from an eighth of an inch, to more than half an inch in
diameter. These, if planted closely, will produce tubers
from four to twelve inches in length, which, although too
small for use, are the most suitable size for planting, to
produce a general crop of medium-sized roots next season.
The ærial tubers are produced in great abundance on some
of the plants, and inconspicuous flowers are also formed
on some of them, of a greenish colour, which I have not
observed to produce any seed.

The plants are said to be bisexual, and if seed could
be procured one drawback in its cultivation might be
remedied by the selection of seedling varieties of the
desired form. The objection referred to, is the great
length to which the roots descend into the earth, which
causes a considerable amount of labour in gathering the
crop. It is singular that although the ærial tubers are
globular, the roots grown from them return to the normal
shape, and accidental roots which are globular, when again
planted do not produce tubers of a similar shape. No
doubt the form of the tuber might be modified to the

M 2

desired extent, if seed could be obtained, by the selection of the shortest roots, continued over a series of generations. However, this defect, which would be objectionable in field culture, on account of the cost of gathering the crop, is, in a garden, no great disadvantage, as it ensures that the portion of the ground in which the Chinese yam is planted, shall be well trenched over in obtaining the roots, and as new ground can be planted every year, in time the whole garden may get a thorough trenching, and thereby get fertilised by exposure to the atmosphere, as well as by the manure which it is convenient to trench into it, at the same time that the crop is gathered.

The largest yam that I have grown was four feet in length, fourteen inches in circumference at the thickest part, and weighed eleven pounds. I re-planted this root whole, and I have not yet examined the root produced this season. It suffered, however, from the heat in summer, which checked its growth. This one was grown in the way practised in the South Sea Islands, where these yams are grown in conical mounds of rich earth, four or five feet high, the runners being allowed to climb up poles placed to support them. The produce of one plant will sometimes be a root five or six feet in length, and as thick as a man's body at the thickest part, being a good load for a wheelbarrow. One such root will serve a family for many weeks, being usually hung up in the native huts, and a slice is cut off every day as required. The size of tuber most convenient for use, is that which is about two inches in diameter. This should be cut in lengths of about four inches, and should be first boiled and then baked until dry and mealy, when it is really delicious, and is preferred by the members of my family to almost any other vegetable. I have grown it in the garden, and used it for nearly thirteen years, having it on the table every day in the season, and it still continues as great a favorite as ever.

I have now the pleasure of laying on the table, for the inspection of the members of the Council, specimens of the tubers in three stages. The first, or smallest specimens, from the size of No. 5 shot, up to the size of a small grape, are the aerial tubers. These, if planted, will in the first year, produce others from four inches to a foot in length, like the second sample. If these are planted, they will produce large-sized tubers, as in the third sample, weighing from one pound to three pounds each. The large specimen is the produce of the third year, from a tuber of about three pounds weight, planted whole. The second year the tuber produced weighed about six pounds; the third year it was four feet long, fourteen inches in circumference at the thickest part, and weighed eleven pounds. The root now laid before you is, unfortunately, forked and divided into three branches and a fourth small one. The whole weighs about fourteen pounds, and the length is three feet eight inches; the circumference of each branch is from eight to nine inches, and of the whole three lying close together sixteen and three-quarter inches. If it had formed a single root, instead of being forked, it would have been a very fine specimen, and it is probably of about the maximum size that the climate will produce, having only increased three pounds over the weight of the set planted. This plant has been grown on a mound of prepared soil about three feet high.

I beg to place these seed bulbs and tubers at the disposal of the council for distribution, should they consider it desirable to disseminate this very useful vegetable, with a view to promote its more extended culture in Victoria.

The original plants of this as well as some roots of the *convolvulus batatas*, or sweet potato, were kindly sent to me many years ago, by a gentleman in Portland, whose name I cannot now recall to memory, or I should take this opportunity of acknowledgment.

I may add, that I have found from my experience in the Wimmera district, that it will thrive and do well in the northern and more arid parts of the colony, where the potato does not stand the climate, and seldom yields even a scanty crop. I have no doubt but that it will suit equally well in Riverina, and more especially in those parts of New South Wales and Queensland, which are favoured with a more copious rainfall than the great plains of the interior of the Australian continent.

GUIDE

Zoological and Acclimatisation Society's Gardens.

BY THE

HON. SECRETARY TO THE SOCIETY.

FIFTH EDITION.

The following description of the Zoological and Acclimatisation Society's Gardens is intended to accompany the bird's-eye view of the grounds in the frontispiece, and may be of some use as a guide to visitors. They comprise an area of about 40 acres, and are situated in the centre of the Royal Park, about a mile and a half from the General Post Office, and can be reached by cab or the Hotham or Brunswick omnibuses, which leave the Hobson's Bay Railway Station every few minutes and take passengers as far as the Park fence on the Flemington or Sydney Road, and within a few minutes' walk of the Gardens.

On entering the main gates the visitor will notice several paths which lead in different directions—with the reader's permission we will proceed round the oval flower bed at the entrance, and so down the main walk for a short distance, until a circular enclosure filled with choice flowers, is reached, which, especially in spring and summer, have a very pleasing effect. The right hand, or opposite side of the walk, is also in the season, gay with flowers and handsome shrubs. From this point several paths again diverge. For the present we will leave the main walk, and turn to the left along an avenue of young Grevillia trees.

On the left hand are two paddocks, No. 1 containing a handsome pair of Alpacas (*Auchenia Pacos*), lately presented to the Society by Mrs. Gellatly, of Elcho ; and in No. 2 are some deer (*Cervus Rusa*), the progenitors of which were sent some years ago to the Society by Sir Henry Barkly, from the Mauritius. They were introduced into that island by the French, from Java, and are now very numerous there. It may here be mentioned that our late respected Governor has always been a warm friend to, and has taken a deep interest in, the Society, and that when here he was an active member of its council.

At the termination of the Grevillia walk, on the left hand, we come to Aviary No. 3. Here we have some Californian Quail introduced by the Society and now rapidly increasing in more than one part of the Colony ; and a pair of Silver Pheasants (*Phasianus Nycthemerus*). In the other division of this Aviary are some beautiful Golden Pheasants (*Phasianus Pictus*), a present from Charles Lyall Grant, Esq., of Shanghai, another staunch friend of the Society ; also some pretty White Doves.

Turning to the right at this point, and passing a private gate (which leads to the residence of the Hon. Secretary) in a few steps we reach Aviary (No. 4), one division of which contains a number of Satin Bower Birds (*Ptilonorhynchus holosericeus*). These birds are very interesting and amusing. In the spring and summer they construct small bowers of light twigs, about two feet in length, and amuse themselves all day in altering the position of the twigs and running through their bower, chasing each other and bowing in the most grotesque manner. The adult males are a glossy purple black, and the young males and females green; but in the male birds the mottled appearance produced by the gradual change of plumage and the intervention of a black feather here and there before the full glossy covering is reached is striking and peculiar. The eye is most beautiful, being of a deep brilliant blue. In the second division of this building are some Turtle Doves (*Turtur Auritus*), which flew on board the good ship *Shannon*, Capt. Stackpool, on a recent voyage to this Port, when off the coast of Portugal. In a third division are a pair of Bleeding Heart Doves (*Calœnæ Luzonica*). Again turning down the Grevillia walk to the left, the visitor passes a paddock (No. 5), devoted to Zebus (or Brahmin Cattle); and also the Kangaroo paddock, tenanted by specimens of the Great Kangaroo (*Macropus Giganteus*); the handsome red Kangaroo (*M. Rufus*) of Riverina, and Bennett's Kangaroo (*Halmaturus Bennetti*) from Tasmania.

Turning to the left at this point along the main walk, the visitor reaches the Cockatoos' Aviary (No. 7), which is filled with those showy, but noisy birds. There are the White Cockatoo (*Cacatua Galerita*), the Corella (*Licmetis Tenuirostris*), Leadbeater's Cockatoo (*Cacatua Leadbeaterii*), the Rose Cockatoo (*Plyctolophus Eos*), and the White Cockatoo of the Solomon Islands (*Cacatua Ophthalmica*). In a separate division are some brilliantly-plumaged Macaws. The Red and Blue (*Ara Araganza*), and the Blue and Yellow (*A. Ararauna*), from Brazil, the latter are a recent acquisition, and were brought out for the Society by Mr. A. H. Jamrach, of London. A little further on is the fountain pond (No. 8), in the centre of the main walk, which is stocked with English Perch and Goldfish; the only birds kept here are some Mandarin Ducks (*Aix Galericulata*), from China.

Again turning to the left as shown on the plan, the visitor is conducted to the large Pheasantry (numbered 11A on the plan), divided into several compartments partly enclosed at the top and partly open. Here several varieties of Pheasants are kept, the breeding of which forms one of the principal features in the Society's operations year by year. The bird found to be the hardiest and best adapted for acclimatising purposes is the ring-necked variety (*Phasianus Torquatus*), known as the New Zealand Pheasant, from the fact of its having been most successfully introduced into that colony. In this Aviary are also some of the curiously marked bleeding-heart Doves (*Calœnas Luzonica*), from Manilla, presented to the Society some years ago by Captain Philip Leigh. In the uncovered portion of this aviary or enclosure are kept some handsome specimens of the Common and White Pea Fowl (*Paro Christatus*).

Partly surrounding the large Pheasantry is a small enclosure (No. 11), in which several Native Companions (*Grus Australasianus*) are confined. These handsome birds are at times very amusing, as they occasionally dance together in the most absurd manner. It is most ridiculous to watch a number of these birds in their wild state dancing in some swamp, as if their very lives depended on it.

On the opposite side of the walk is the small Mammals house (No. 10), containing at present a fine collection of Opossums, small Flying Squirrels, Native Cats, Kangaroo Rats, the Blotched Genett, the Moongus, and other small animals.

A few yards to the right is the Bear-pit (No. 12), inhabited by a specimen of the North American bear (*Ursus Americanus*); the orthodox pole rises in the centre, but its occupant is so well fed and lazy, that he seldom takes the trouble to climb it.

Close by, at the foot of an old gum tree (No. 13), a fine specimen of the Yellow Fox (*Vulpes Flavescens*) is kept; and on the other side of the walk is another small paddock (No. 9) for birds.

Still following the same path, the visitor next reaches two buildings (Nos. 14 and 15), placed on each side of the main walk, in which are confined both birds and beasts. In No. 14 are two fine specimens of the Native Dog (*Canis Dingo*), a Silver-backed Jackal (*Canis Mesomelas*), and a pair of those hideous animals, the Tasmanian Devil (*Sarcophilus Ursinus*), the latter in a cage made additionally strong to prevent their escape, as there are few animals in the world which possess the same strength in proportion to their size. In the centre and corner cages are a number of beautiful Parrots, and a fine specimen of the Kakapo, or Night Owl Parrot of New Zealand.

No. 15 contains a fine Striped Hyæna, a Racoon (*Procyon Lotor*), and a pair of Marsupial Wolves or Native Tigers (*Thylacinus Cynocephalus*) from Tasmania. Like the Dingo, these animals are very destructive to sheep, and they have in consequence been destroyed by the settlers, and are now becoming scarce. Several Monkeys are also kept here, and, as in No. 14, a number of Parrots in the corner cages.

Near to these cages at the end of the Main Walk are the Deer paddocks. (Nos. 16, 17, 18, and 19). These enclosures, as will be seen on the plan, extend across the whole breadth of the grounds. They contain a number of Deer of the following varieties:—

The Formosan Deer (*Cervus Pseudaxis*). Formosa, a beautiful spotted Deer, the first of which were presented to the Society by R. S. Fussell, Esq., of Fou Chou.

The Japanese Deer (*C. Sika*).—This variety is very like the Formosan, being also spotted; but it is a smaller animal.

The Barasingha Deer (*C. Duvaucelli*), Northern India.—Presented by Arthur Grote, Esq., late of Calcutta. This Deer attains a large size.

The Sambur Deer (*C. Aristotelis*), India.—Some years ago several of these fine animals were liberated at Harewood, near Cranbourne, the property of William Lyall, Esq., and have increased in a remarkable manner. Mr. Lyall estimates that there are now some hundreds running on a large swamp on his station.

The Fallow Deer (*C. Dama*), Europe.—At present there are only two females in the Gardens, but there are numbers in different parts of the colony, notably on the Upper Yarra, the produce of some liberated several years ago by P. De Castella, Esq.

The Hog Deer (*C. Porcinus*), India.—This is a small, hardy animal, about the size of a sheep. A number have been liberated at different times. The original stock was presented by the Rajah

Rajendro Mullick, Messrs. E. Blythe and A. Grote, of Calcutta, and A. Layard, Esq., of Colombo.

The Axis Deer (*C. Axis*), India, have also been introduced by the Society, and are very numerous in the neighbourhood of the Grampians.

The New Lion House (No. 20) is situated in one of the Deer paddocks (No. 19). It is a handsome structure, built of brick, on a solid bluestone foundation, with substantial iron front, and has been completed at a considerable cost. The centre compartment contains a splendid pair of South African Lions (*Felis Leo*); the other compartments contain a young Lioness, their daughter, born in the Gardens, and now about two years old, and a young Tigress (*Felis Tigris*), presented to the Society by The Hon. T. J. Sumner, M.L.C. The Carnivora are fed daily (Sundays excepted) at half-past three o'clock. A little further on along the same path brings the visitor to a wooden cage (No. 21), containing a large Chacma Baboon (*Cynocephalus Porcarius*): this animal was formerly kept on the chain, but as he managed to break it on several occasions and make his escape, it was thought better and safer to confine him.

The visitor now turns to the right hand, and to the left of the path is the Emu paddock (No. 22), in which are several of these fine birds and a young one hatched this season. There is also a Brahmin Cow and Calf, in this paddock.

The next building (No. 23) is the old Lion House. It contains a Hunting Leopard or Cheetah (*Felis Jubata*), a fine Panther (*Leopardus Varius*), the Black Leopard (*Felis Nigra*), and the Common Leopard (*Felis Leopardus*), the latter recently presented to the Society by His Excellency Sir William Gregory, late Governor of Ceylon.

From this point, as the turnings are numerous, the visitor had better refer to the plan for further guidance.

No. 24 is the next in order, and is the largest Aviary in the Garden. A number of beautiful birds are collected here, viz.:—

The Golden Pheasant (*Phasianus Pictus*).
Bleeding-heart Doves (*Calænas Luzonica*).
The Wonga Wonga Pigeon (*Leucosarcia Picata*).
The Great Crowned Pigeon (*Gaura Coronata*), from New Guinea, and a number of smaller birds.

A little further on, and the Song Bird Aviary (No. 25) is reached, filled with Canaries, Linnets, and Goldfinches, &c., which make melody the whole day long. In the winter months it is, however, occasionally necessary to move the birds to warmer quarters,

No. 26. The Native Bear Tree. In which one of these singular animals (*Phascolarctus Cinereus*) lives for the greater part of the year, though occasionally he denudes his abode so entirely of leaves that he has to be removed to another tree for a time. It has hitherto been found impossible to take specimens of these singular and interesting animals to Europe, as they require a constant supply of fresh gum leaves to feed on, and even then, if confined in a cage, they will not live for any length of time. The only way of keeping them successfully is to put them up a gum-tree. They have a most peculiar cry, something between the grunting of a pig and the crying of a child. Of all the doleful sounds which break the stillness of night in the Australian bush, there is none so unearthly as that of the Bear. Within the close fence at the foot of the tree the Porcupine Anteaters (*Echidna Hystrix*) are kept; sometimes there are several, and at other times not a single specimen in the collection, for they are difficult creatures to keep alive for any length of time in confinement.

No. 27. The Wombat's Cave. There are two specimens of this curious animal, one black and one grey, (*Phascolomys Platyrhinus*) at present in the Society's possession, but they study their own comfort more than the curiosity of visitors, and generally remain coiled up in their den during the day; for like many of the Australian animals, they are nocturnal, and in their wild state only feed at night.

No. 28. The Reptile house. Recently added to the attractions of the Gardens. It contains a fine Boa Constrictor,* recently received from the Zoological Gardens of Batavia, and several cases, in one of which are brown banded or Tiger Snakes (*Hoplocephalus Curtus*), and Black Snakes (*Pseudechis Porphyriacus*), the larged-scaled Snake (*Hoplocephalus Superbus*), and the Brown Snake—all highly venomous, especially the first three varieties. In another case are some Diamond Snakes (*Morelia Spilotes*), from New South Wales, and a couple of Carpet Snakes (*Morelia Variegata*), from Riverina—both these varieties are harmless. There is also a case containing an Iguana or Coast Lizard (*Hydrosaurus Varius*), and a case of Lizards of different kinds.

Nos. 29 and 30. The Waterfowl Ponds. The present collection consists of—

Magpie Geese (*Anseranas Melanoleuca*).
Egyptian Geese (*Chenalopex Ægyptiaca*).

---

* This Reptile has since died.

Cape Barren Geese (*Cereopsis Novæ Hollandiæ*).

Canadian Geese (*Anser Canadensis*).

Maned Geese (*Bernicla Jubata*).

Bar-headed Geese (*Anser Indicus*).

Chinese Geese (*Anser Cygnoides*).

The Mute Swan (*Cygnus Olor*).

The Black Swan (*C. Atratus*).

The Shieldrake or Mountain Duck (*Casarca Tadornoides*).

The Paradise Duck, from New Zealand (*C. Variegata*).

The Black Indian Duck.

The Mallard (*Anas Boschas*).

The Australian Black Duck (*Anas Superciliosa*).

        &c.   &c.

No. 31. The Smaller Pheasantry, which contains the ring-necked variety (*Phasianus Torquatus*), the Japanese green (*P. Versicolor*), and a pair of Copper Pheasants (*P. Sæmmeringhii*). The two last named were given to the Society by Charles Lyall Grant, Esq., of Shanghai, and are probably the only representatives of their kind at present in Australia.

No. 32 is a small paddock in which are several Land Tortoises from Southern Africa, the largest of which was presented to the Society by His Excellency Sir George Bowen. Within this enclosure, but fenced off, are several Baboons and other Monkeys, all provided with small houses and poles in front, up which they delight to climb. The antics of these animals, cause many a hearty laugh to the old as well as to the young.

Opposite to this paddock are four small cages filled with Monkeys (marked No. 33 in the plan), and close by a Circular Aviary (No. 34), which contains a collection of different kinds of birds. There are some fine specimens of the Australian Eagle (*Aquila Audax*); the Laughing Jackass (*Dacelo Gigas*); the English Raven (*Corvus Corax*); the Weeka Rail (*Ocydromys Australis*), New Zealand; the Kagu (*Rhinochetus Jubatus*), New Caledonia; the Horned Owl (*Bubo Bengalensis*), India; the Chesnut-faced Owl (*Strix Castanops*), Tasmania; the South Stone Plover (*Ædicnemus Grallarius*); the White Hawk (*Astur Novæ Hollandiæ*), and other birds.

No 35. The Wallaby Paddock. There are several varieties of these pretty little animals in the Society's collection, all of which breed regularly. Foremost among them is the Yellow-footed Rock Wallaby (*Petrogale Xanthopus*) of South Australia; it is of a light brown color, very prettily marked, and its long tail is striped or barred like a tiger's. Then come the Gloved Wallaby (*Halmaturus Manicatus*), the Brush-tailed Wallaby (*Halmaturus Ualabatus*), and the Paddy-melon (*Halmaturus Billardieri*), the latter generally found in the salt bush country.

No. 36. A small enclosure, in which are several Native Turkeys or Bustards (*Otis Australasianus*).

No. 37. The Refreshment Room. Which is in the occupation of Mr. W. Strickland of Brunswick, and has proved a great convenience to visitors.

It is intended shortly to enlarge the Reptile House, and to erect a new cage for the Hyæna, who at present is poorly provided for. Further additions to the collection are expected from the Zoological Society of Batavia, and the Council of the Society is determined to spare no effort to keep up and add to the attractions of the Gardens.

www.ingramcontent.com/pod-product-compliance
Lightning Source LLC
Chambersburg PA
CBHW030839270326
41928CB00007B/1121